GILBERT & GEORGE

THE PARADISICAL PICTURES

THE GILBERT & GEORGE CENTRE

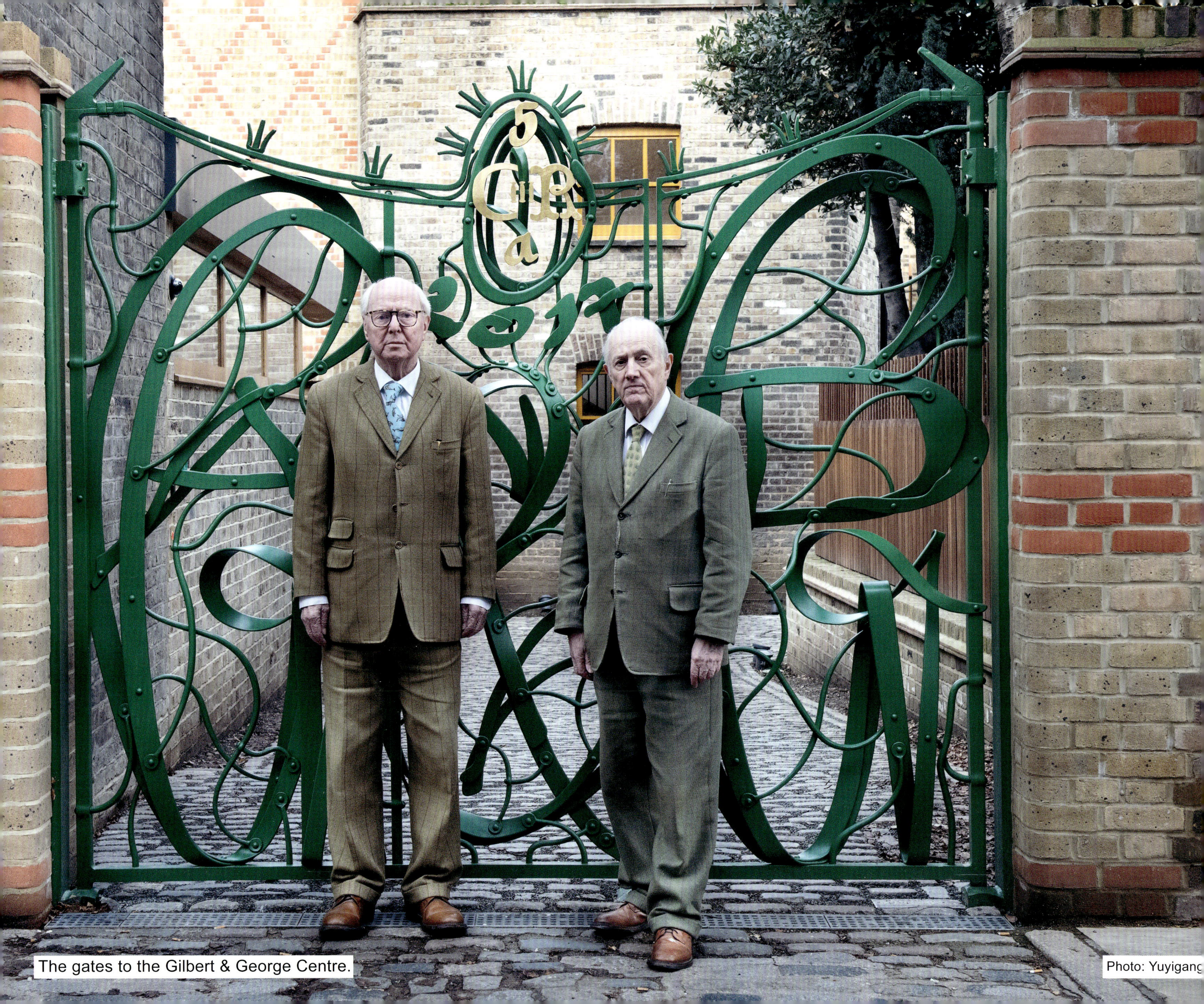

The gates to the Gilbert & George Centre.

Photo: Yuyigang

GILBERT & GEORGE

THE PARADISICAL PICTURES

THE GILBERT & GEORGE CENTRE

2023

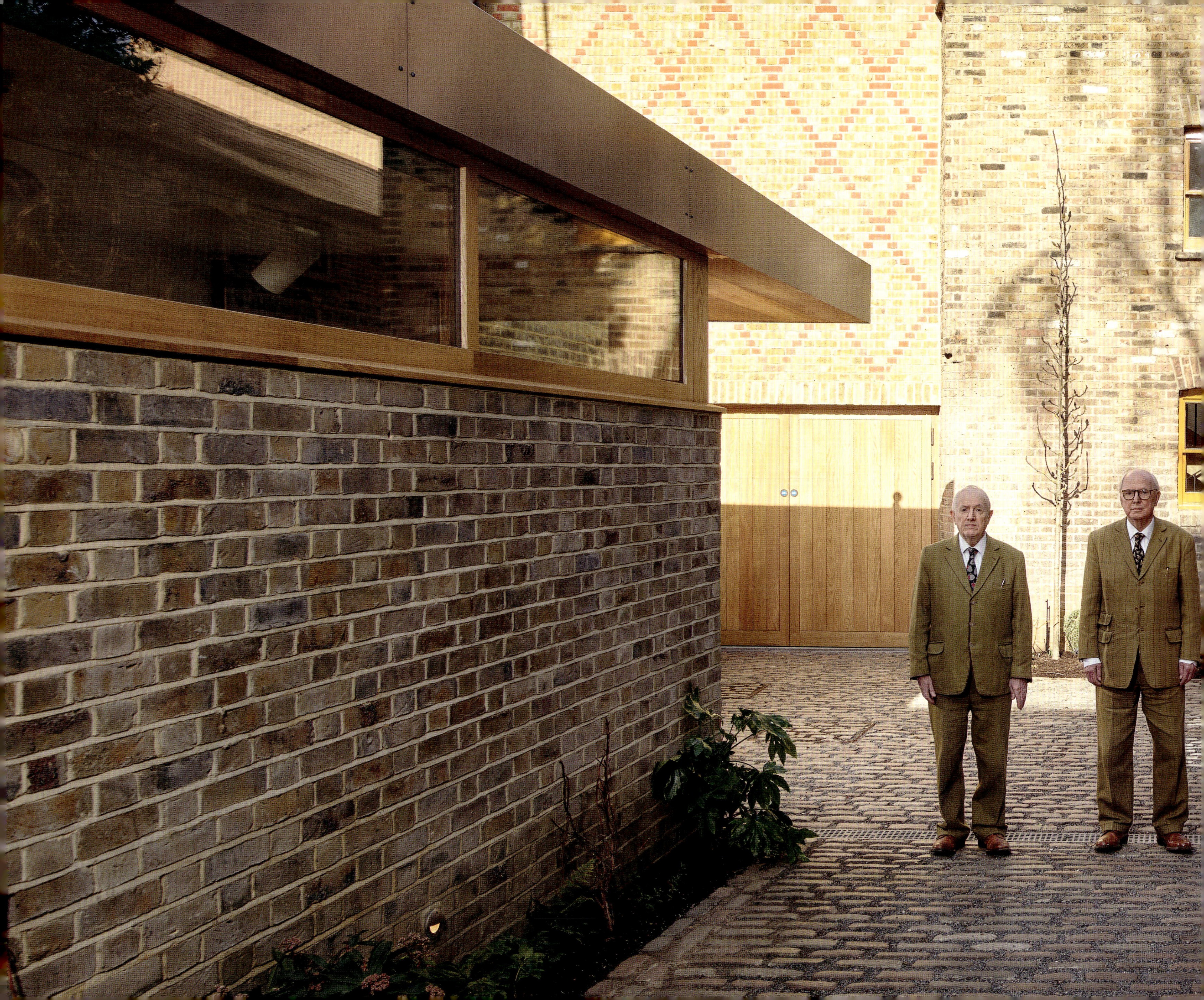

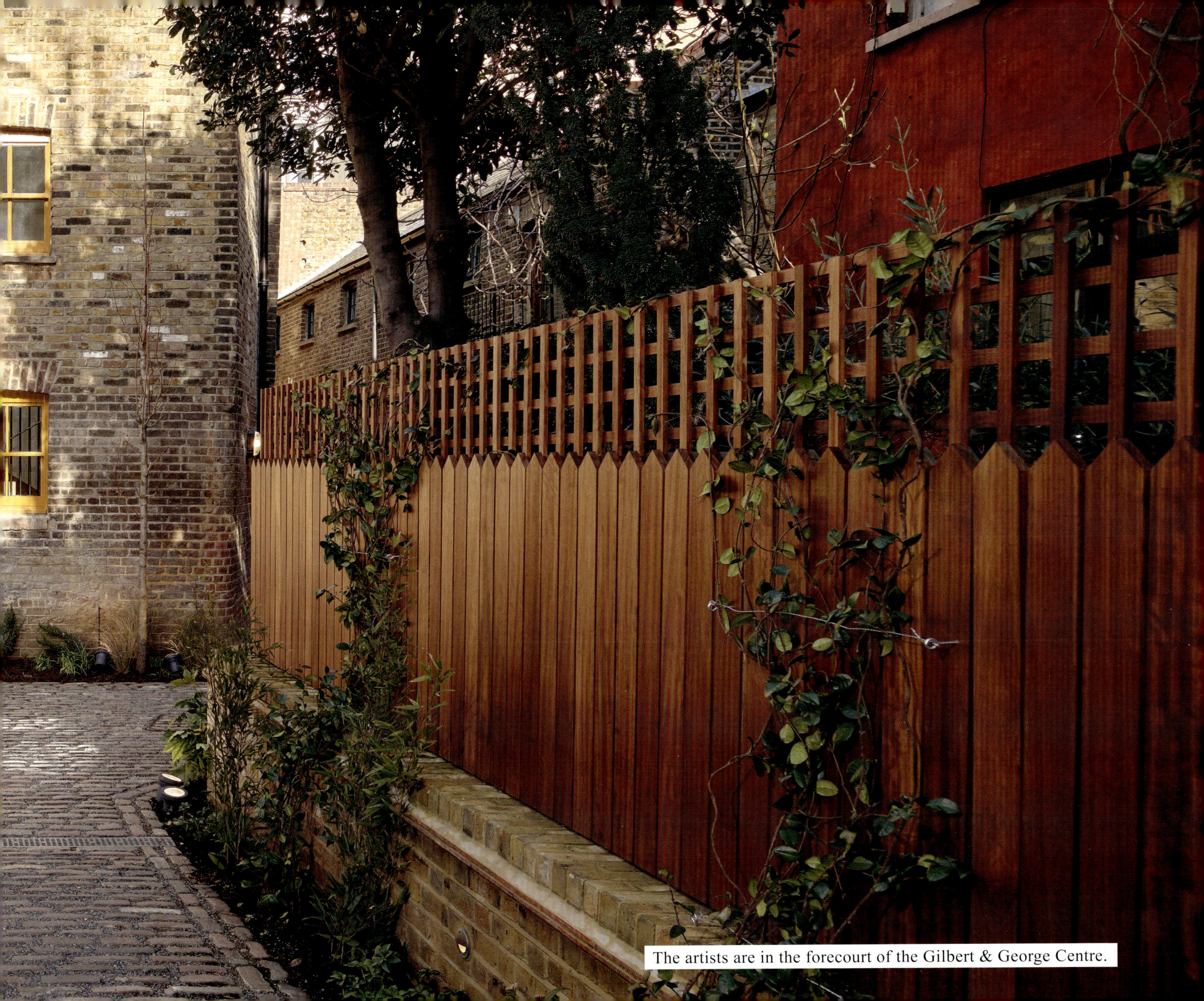

The artists are in the forecourt of the Gilbert & George Centre.

THE PARADISICAL PICTURES EXHIBITION

ANTHERS
LEFT BEHIND
ROSY
ROSEMANCE
DARWIN DAY
BED-WETTING
DATE RAPE
COTTAGE GARDEN
TENDER
FULL FIG
PET
EATEN MESS

DATE STONES
CHAIN BRAIN
REST
DATE DANCE
THRICE
LION TEETH
SEXPARTITE
MAGNOLIA HEADS
ON THE BENCH
DENT-DE-LION
GOLD BASKET

BOOTS
CURL
DATE FUCK
DATE STONE FUCK
LICHEN DAYS
CHAINS
CHAINERY
FIGGED
GROVE
DATE STONE HEADS
GREENLY
DATE HEADS

THE PARADISICAL PICTURES

and the Art of Gilbert & George

Michael Bracewell

2022

A group of the dazzling and disquieting PARADISICAL PICTURES are the first to be shown by Gilbert & George at *The Gilbert & George Centre*. This historic exhibition presents the art of Gilbert & George at its most hallucinogenic and uncompromising.

Two men like the ghosts of old-style vaudevillians, dressed in varicoloured matching suits with collar and tie, pose in dead-eyed attitudes of shock and exhaustion within a violently coloured jungle world of monstrous decaying blossoms and vegetation. Their expressions are vacant, locked in dream-state. Here, they dance a zombie-dance; there, they gaze transfixed, empty-headed, or confronted deep within themselves by some new vision. Then these men stare up at us with red demonic eyes. It looks as though they are drowning in a whirlpool of dead flowers; they become body shapes made of chain, their faces appear on date stones; and here they stand before us, in a formal pose, straight-backed, like other-worldly librarians, middle-managers of the dead, returning our gaze. They are stern and severe.

They look as though they are regarding us from another dimension. In their suits and ties – uniforms of respectable responsibility – they stand surrounded by giant flowers, by roses and their thorny stems, the petals of which are fleshy and wilting in sickly toxic shades of acid green, dusty pink, puce, scarlet, mauve.

Such is the world of the thirty five PARADISICAL PICTURES made by Gilbert & George in 2019. It is a world in which atmosphere doubles as event – a quality shared with the films of Alfred Hitchcock or early animated films by Walt Disney studios. Their heightened, saturated, violent, cloying colours convey hallucinogenic portent, unease – like musty-sweet sleeping gas.

Gilbert & George take their place in this disquieting vision of a heavenly place in a manner resembling psychical reports or transmissions from a journey deep into an enchanted forest or overgrown park. It is a psychedelic landscape, as though the pre-Raphaelite artists of the mid-nineteenth century, more given to poetic realism and Arthurian legend, had secretly envisioned science-fiction. The disembodied eyes of Gilbert & George stare unnervingly through tangles of fluorescent briars, reminiscent of the effigies of Green Men nature spirits superstitiously admitted into the decoration of churches by medieval stone masons.

This particular paradise – paradise being the common goal of spiritual and secular life on Earth – inhabited or traversed by Gilbert & George, is a place where the very air is drugged. From picture to picture, the artists are subject to biomorphic alteration into vegetable states – a turn of events that would be cartoon-like and absurd were it not so equally sinister. The dead yet watchful eyes of Gilbert & George stare sleeplessly from grotesque detritus of fruits and flowers; from masks of dead leaves – details of spirit faces, as the artists themselves are seen first pursued by unseen wonders or horrors, then finally exhausted, worn out, in a sleep that seems to promise no rest.

The longer you look at these PARADISICAL PICTURES, the more they suggest a chapter in a story that has been unfolding before them and will continue beyond them. This paradise is not a destination but a stage on a longer journey. It is a dream of paradise – the exploration of an archetype; to be granted bliss, eternal rest, true life, revelation, the answer to life's mysteries. The paradise of these PARADISICAL PICTURES, however, proposes a more ambivalent view – a place of mutation, exhaustion, watchfulness and possession: an empty promise. The viewer must decide.

But the paradise explored in the PARADISICAL PICTURES is historically linked to the earlier stages on the visionary journey of Gilbert & George. In the charcoal-on-paper sculptures of the early 1970s, such as THERE WERE TWO YOUNG MEN or THE GENERAL JUNGLE, the viewer sees Gilbert & George when they were young men, surrounded by nature – conversing, walking, relaxing. The countryside appears gentler, more mannered – a prelapsarian state of youth. Nearly fifty years later, the jungle garden seems darker and stranger, the travellers close to exhaustion…

The art of Gilbert & George confounds and rejects all art historical classification or affiliation to other schools or movements in art. As evidenced by these PARADISICAL PICTURES, there is no formalist, aesthetic or conceptual precedent to the ideology and vision they convey with such intensity. They are fantastical, allegorical, narrative, representational, psychedelic, absurdist, modern yet archaic, surrealist-grotesque, inflected with both tragedy and comedy, filled with pathos, touchingly eloquent of human frailty, age and exhaustion. They suggest a philosophy but do not dictate its tenets. In short, the art of Gilbert & George is a *visionary* art, above all – reports from a long journey through life, emotional, spiritual, psychical, cosmic, that begins on the streets of London…

Gilbert & George are two men who together are one artist. Gilbert is from the Dolomites region of northern Italy. George from Devon, England. They met in September 1967 when they were both students in what was then the internationally acclaimed Sculpture Department at St Martin's School of Art, London. The relationship between the two young men was immediate, profound and absolute – 'Love at first sight', as they have said.

From the very beginning of their life together, Gilbert & George would wander the streets of London, district by district; far from the fashionable and 'artistic' West End, or bohemian Notting Hill, and through the ancient and modern alleys and courtyards of the financial City – in those days part Dickensian, part concrete Brutalism; then off to the east, south and north – to remote Victorian suburbs, derelict missions and slumbering slums: to the sprawling East End, the silent old Docklands; riding obscure buses up to Wood Green, Finsbury and Tottenham, or down to Streatham or Norbury. They were always together and always alone, absorbing the past, present and future of London's immensity, searching for a vision of art.

Having moved to what were then the slums and desolation of East London, and having nothing but each other and the streets they walked, Gilbert & George then realised – had the life-changing revelation – that *they* were their art. They named themselves Living Sculptures and dedicated their lives to the ceaseless, arduous, all-consuming task of being Gilbert & George. They were their own medium, unique. They needed nobody and nothing.

Their beliefs and activities as artists, appropriating forms of conservatism and traditionalism (then regarded as artistically, ideologically heretical) to their own radically Romantic ends, were opposed to those of their tutors and contemporaries. They dressed like archaic bank clerks – suited, with neat haircuts, as formal and polite as young seminarians.

Gilbert & George had a vision and mission as artists, however, that was both framed and amplified by their sartorial conservatism and demeanour. For their art was dedicated to the direct communication of extreme states of feeling and being: to the debased, outcast, drunken, solitary, ignored, looked-down upon, explicit, bodily, commonplace, violent and vulgar. The more formal, polite and mild-mannered Gilbert & George presented themselves, the more confrontational, stark, emotional and uncompromising their art and subject matter became.

In the vision and art of Gilbert & George – as embodied by Gilbert & George – the reactionary became radicalised. The art of Gilbert & George was thus the reverse of contemporary art as it was usually received. And in this reversal it was avant-garde, in the original meaning of that term, as 'agent of reform'.

Rejecting all schools of contemporary artistic practice – preferring and asserting the radicalism of mid-Victorian artists and architects – Gilbert & George established a form of phantasmagorical realism, in which intense romanticism was combined with brutal urban realism. They likewise rejected irony, intellectualism, politics, formalism, conceptualism and all other mainstays of contemporary art, as decadent, elitist and irrelevant to anyone outside the small humid village of the 'art world'.

As reversal is said to be a mainstay of practical magic, so this reversal of contemporary artistic vision, ideals and values conjured into being the single and singular artist, Gilbert & George. From the moment of this realisation, Gilbert & George had known their transformation into the single artist Gilbert & George was absolute and complete. Gilbert & George were born therefore of opposition and reversal as avant-garde traditionalist revolutionaries, embarking on a lifetime's spiritual journey.

The art of Gilbert & George is best summarised, therefore, as the *vision* of Gilbert & George – as a creed and an ideology that is also a method and a principle. This vision is their experience and celebration of life, and simultaneously their way of seeing and making art. On their walks around London and more locally around their home in Spitalfields, Gilbert & George saw the modern human condition: acceleration, religion, politics, business, boredom, leisure, celebration, violence, money, history, poverty, age, sex, work, hope, newness, sickness, desire, intoxication, beauty, dereliction, love, despair; the radicalised world; the virtual world.

They saw the daily routines and feelings of their fellow citizens, from all backgrounds: the fast modern multicultural and multi-technological world. Office workers, cycle couriers, builders and junkies; the spectrum of human behaviour. They observed the constantly changing life of the city the way one might observe the weather, or study the ceaseless current of a vast river.

Artistically, their vision found heightened or disturbed emotion in ordinary things, in a way that rendered the apparently commonplace subjects of their art extraordinary and richly atmospheric: mysterious and meaningful, individual, yet connected by common feelings. The dramatic impact of their art derived from this union of lucid realism and intense emotion; from the balance, psychologically and artistically (in the studio) of control and loss of control.

The artistic vision of Gilbert & George has always been based on what the artists define as 'the moral dimension' in their Art. This moral dimension relates the imprint of time and human activity on all things. Gilbert & George have described how the subject matter of their art and of each group of new pictures only reveals itself when they have recognised and experienced its particular moral dimension. Their art conveys the strange, alluring eloquence of the imprint of time, nature and humanity – its metaphysical and quotidian truth.

The moral dimension in the art of Gilbert & George is powerfully empathetic, as though all phenomena were sentient: the sadness of an old wall; the desire of the leaves, the personalities of street names, the temper of graffiti or the loneliness of broken glass. In the art of Gilbert & George all things become archetypical, a cosmic-realist landscape of living symbols: litter, traffic, drunkenness, clowning or clouds; anonymous youths, luxuriant or dead flowers, snow, advertisements for sex workers, old statues, newspaper headlines. All of the image-subjects in the art of Gilbert & George configure to create fantastical tableaux: vertiginous, declamatory, elegiac, absurdist, crazy, lucid-dreaming scenes of modern life.

The artists have defined their art as visionary, in the manner of William Blake, and likened its course since the late 1960s to a modern *Pilgrim's Progress*; a mystical-visionary journey through life, in which spiritual allegory and unyielding realism are entwined and interrelated. The most efficient and direct communication through their art, pictorially and technically, of these truths and this visionary journey comprises the ideology of Gilbert & George.

The viewer experiences the drama, temper or strangeness of the art of Gilbert & George as though looking through a portal into a Wonderland or a parallel dimension within our common reality; a place where archetypes and symbols create their own strange pageantry: the rain, the street, the psychic force-field of a million strangers; the collapse of meaning into primal forces. It is an art which speaks directly and lovingly to the broadest number of people, regardless of their nationality, faith, political views or sexuality. To use their own term, Gilbert & George make ART FOR ALL.

And as Gilbert & George make their ART FOR ALL, so their art is about us all. The universality of the human condition is the constant, principal subject in the art of Gilbert & George; that despite the impositions of boundaries, frontiers, religions, ideologies and language, there is a deeper democracy of physical and psychological realities. Love, anger, hope, pride, loneliness, desire, illness, despair, fear, boredom, inspiration and joy are universal, as surely as old age and mortality. Thus the moral vision of Gilbert & George relates the corporeal facts of existence to our experience within the natural, cosmic and spiritual worlds, as well as the modern city.

The art of Gilbert & George has always addressed the existential condition of living in a modern, technological, multi-sexual, multi-faith, multicultural society – they are, historically and fundamentally, the most diversity and inclusivity aware artists working today. Their work is filled with the human presence of a myriad beliefs and cultures, from western capitalism to Muslim, Jewish, Hindu, Christian or Sikh, anarchists, agnostics, commuters, tourists, workers and outcasts. The social and cultural landscape, in fact, of modern East London.

Since the late 1960s, Gilbert & George have shared their lives – their spiritual progress – with the viewer through their art. From the earliest days, they politely invited the viewer to accompany them – to share the experience of their vision: in walks through nature, in bars and pubs, in the bleak morning light, on dark streets, in vividly coloured visionary vistas, in the strange countries of their own body fluids; and then it seemed, as though through some form of death and reincarnation; thence to more of a ghost world – through several purgatories, of daily tragedy, of paranoia, of anarchy, of masks and barbed wire, the borders closing; and now the fluorescent paradisical dream jungle.

Gilbert & George politely invite their friends, the viewers, into this maelstrom.

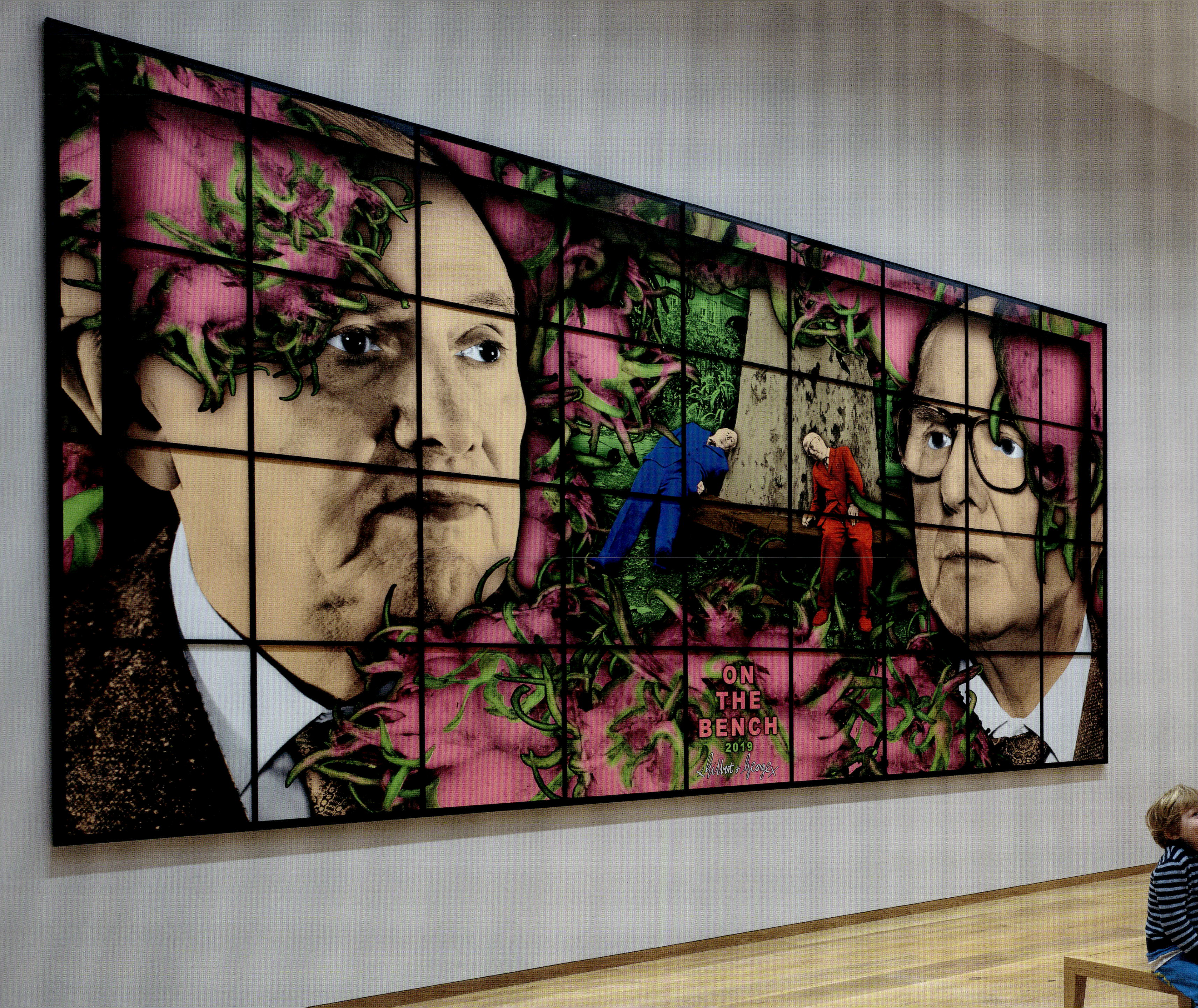
ON
THE
BENCH
2019

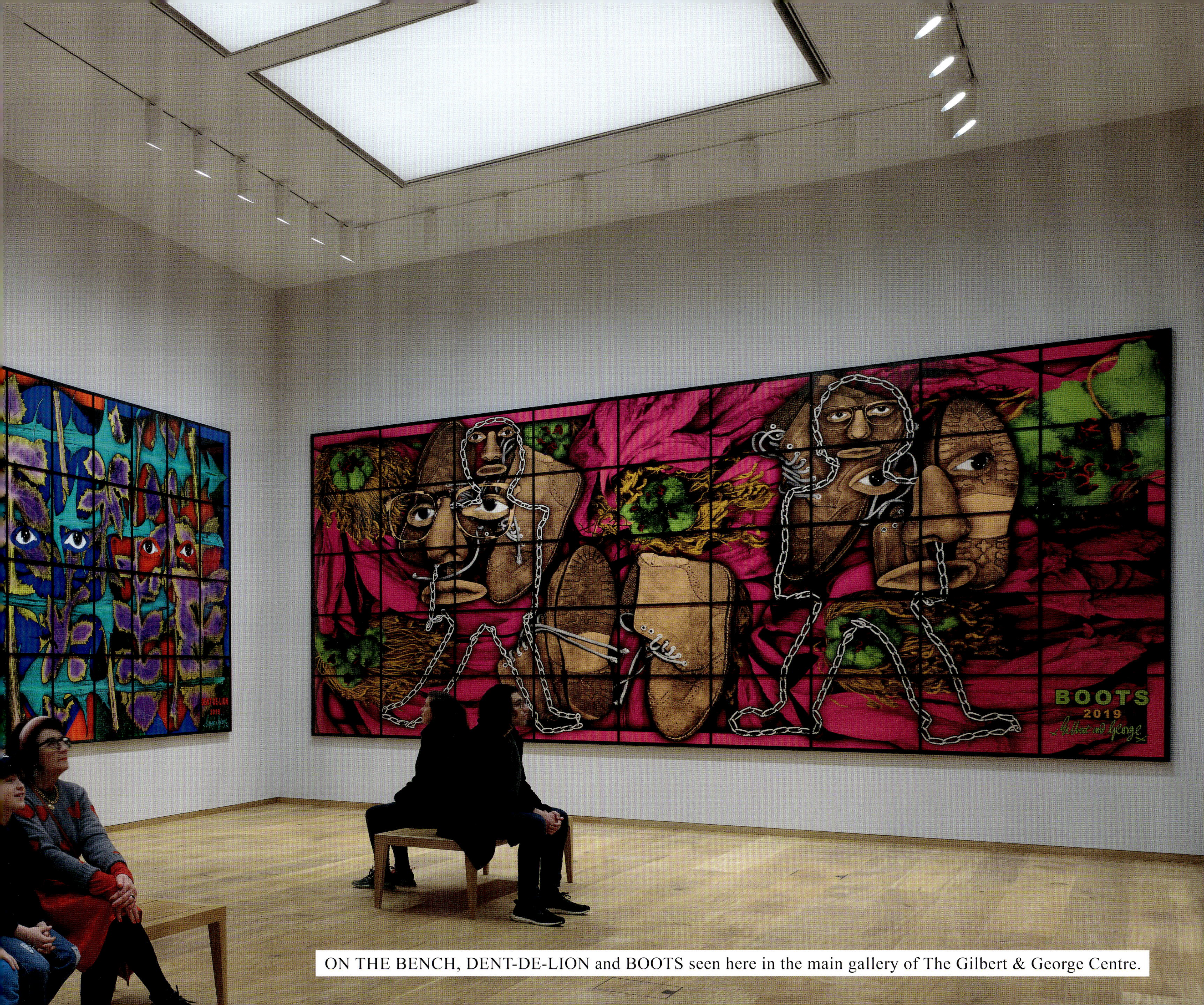

ON THE BENCH, DENT-DE-LION and BOOTS seen here in the main gallery of The Gilbert & George Centre.

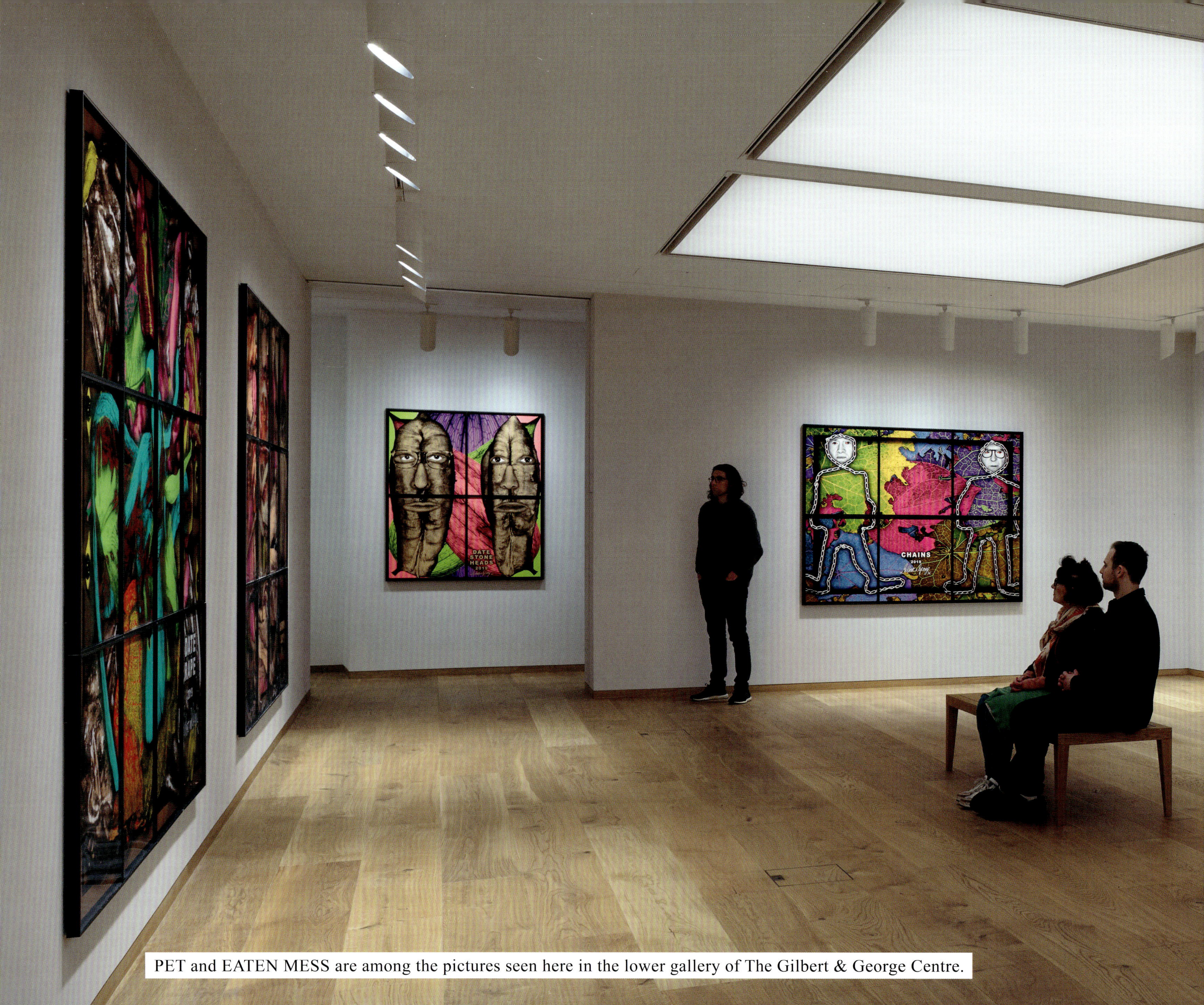

PET and EATEN MESS are among the pictures seen here in the lower gallery of The Gilbert & George Centre.

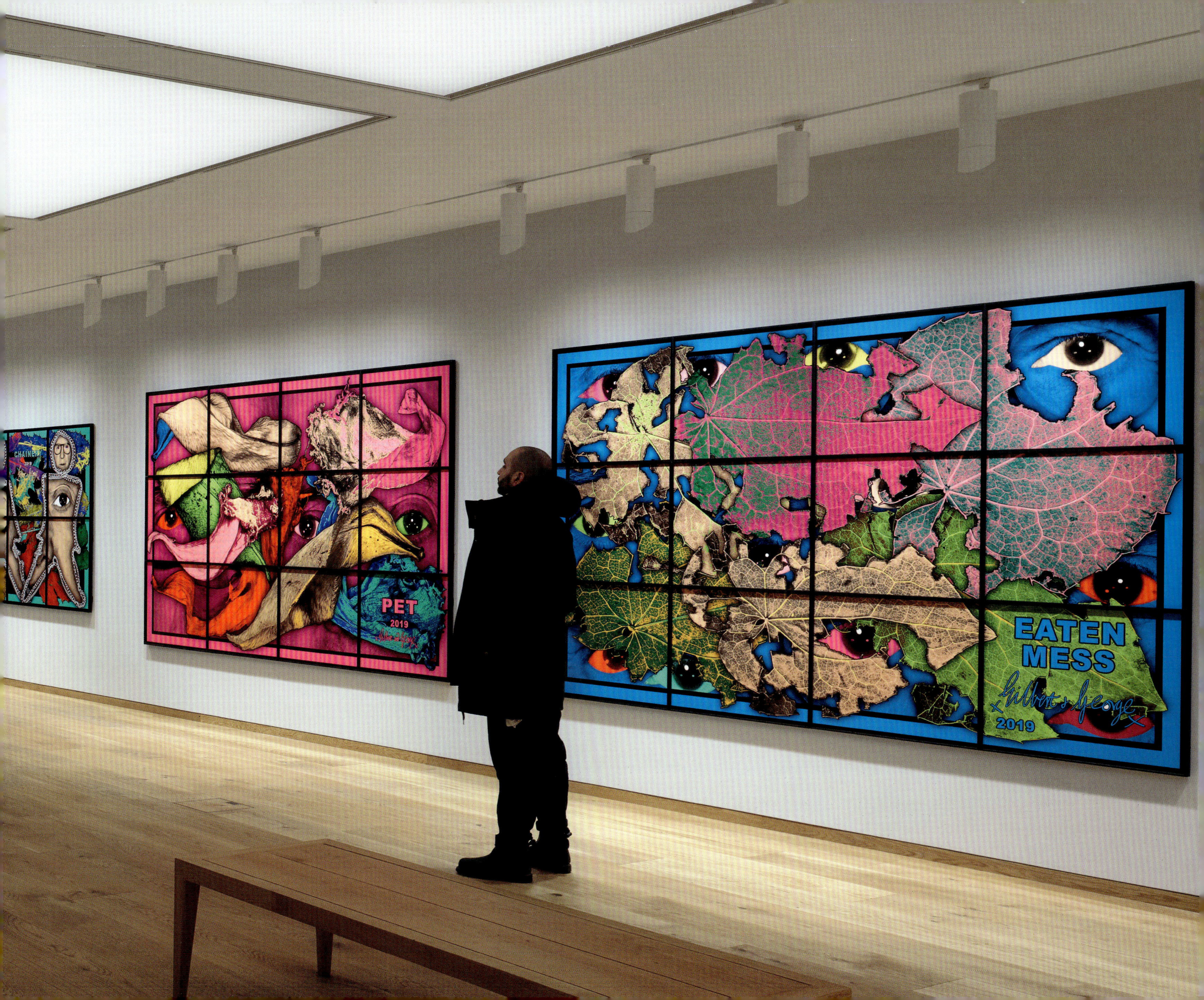
PET
2019
EATEN
MESS
Gilbert & George
2019

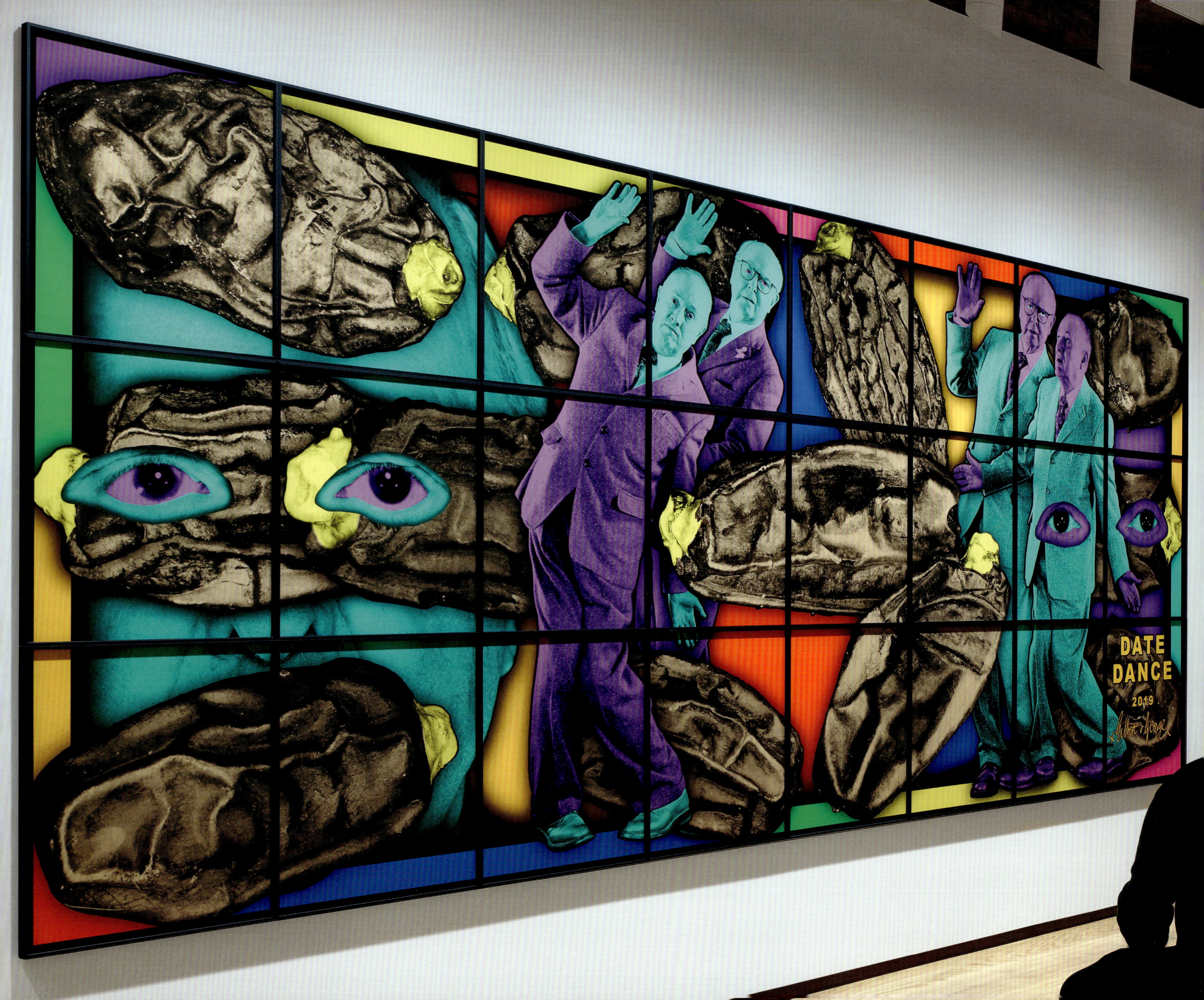
DATE
DANCE
2019

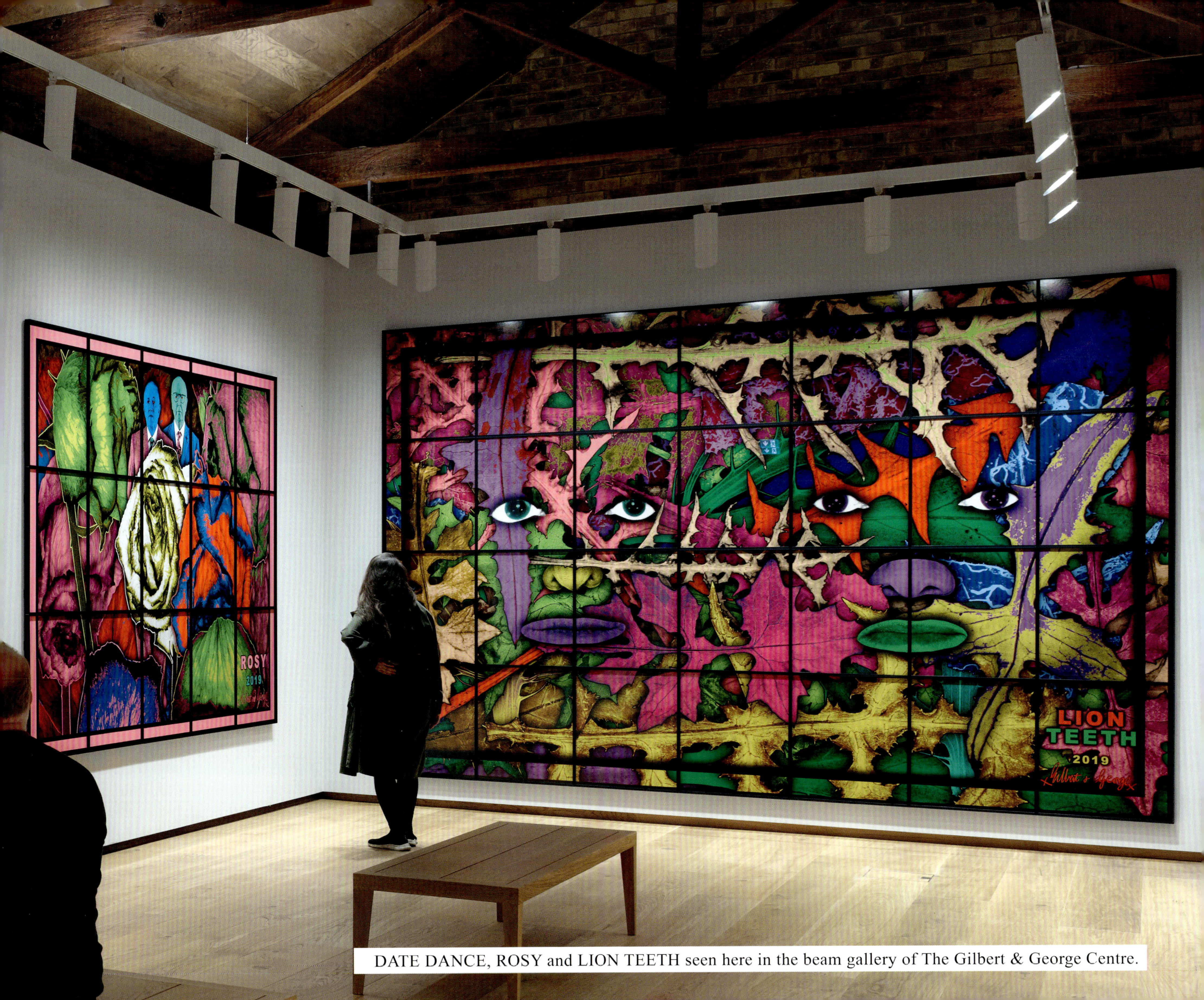

DATE DANCE, ROSY and LION TEETH seen here in the beam gallery of The Gilbert & George Centre.

THE PARADISICAL PICTURES

2019

Reproduced here in the order in which they were created

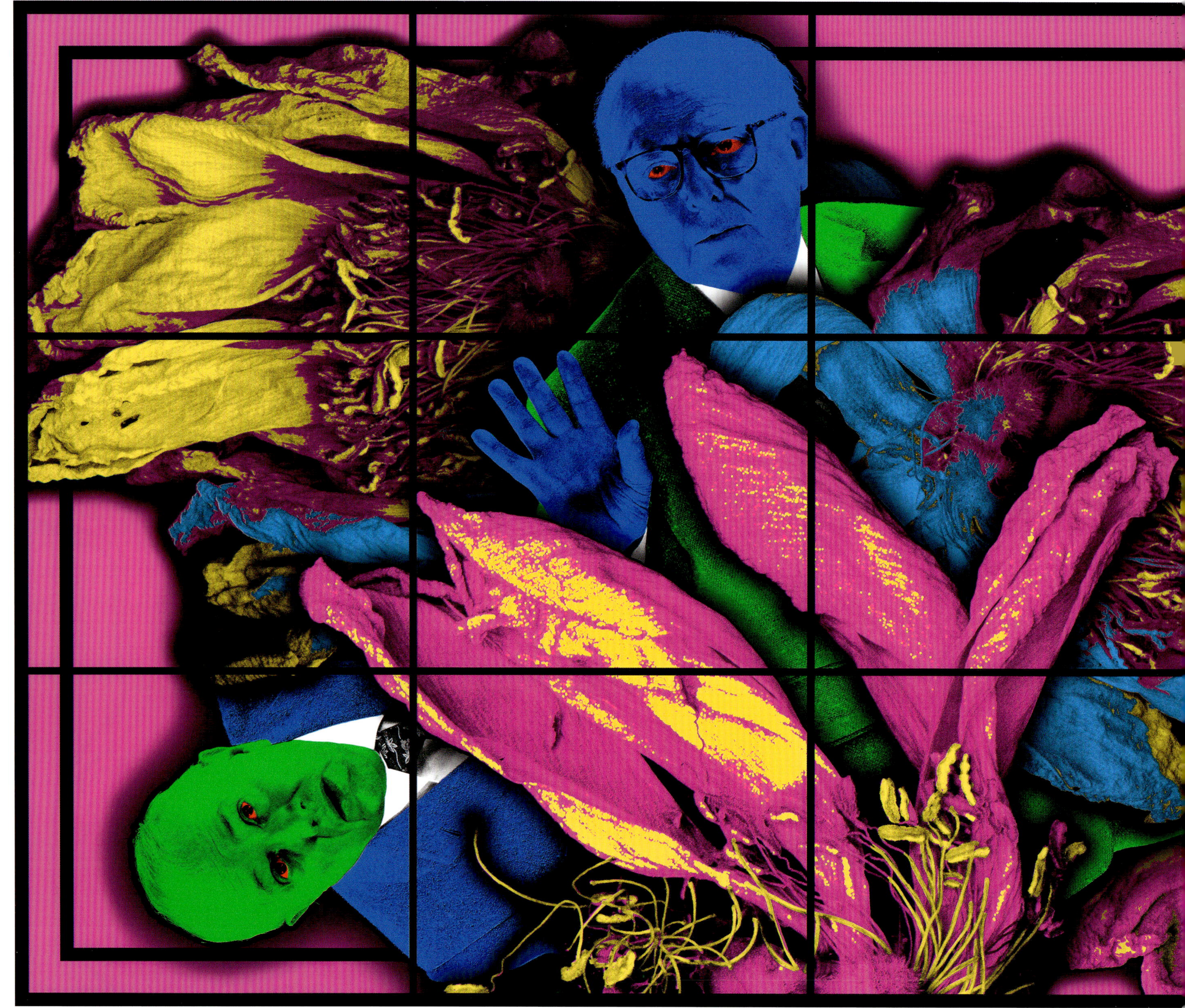

ANTHERS. 2019. 75 x 178 inches (190 x 451 cm)

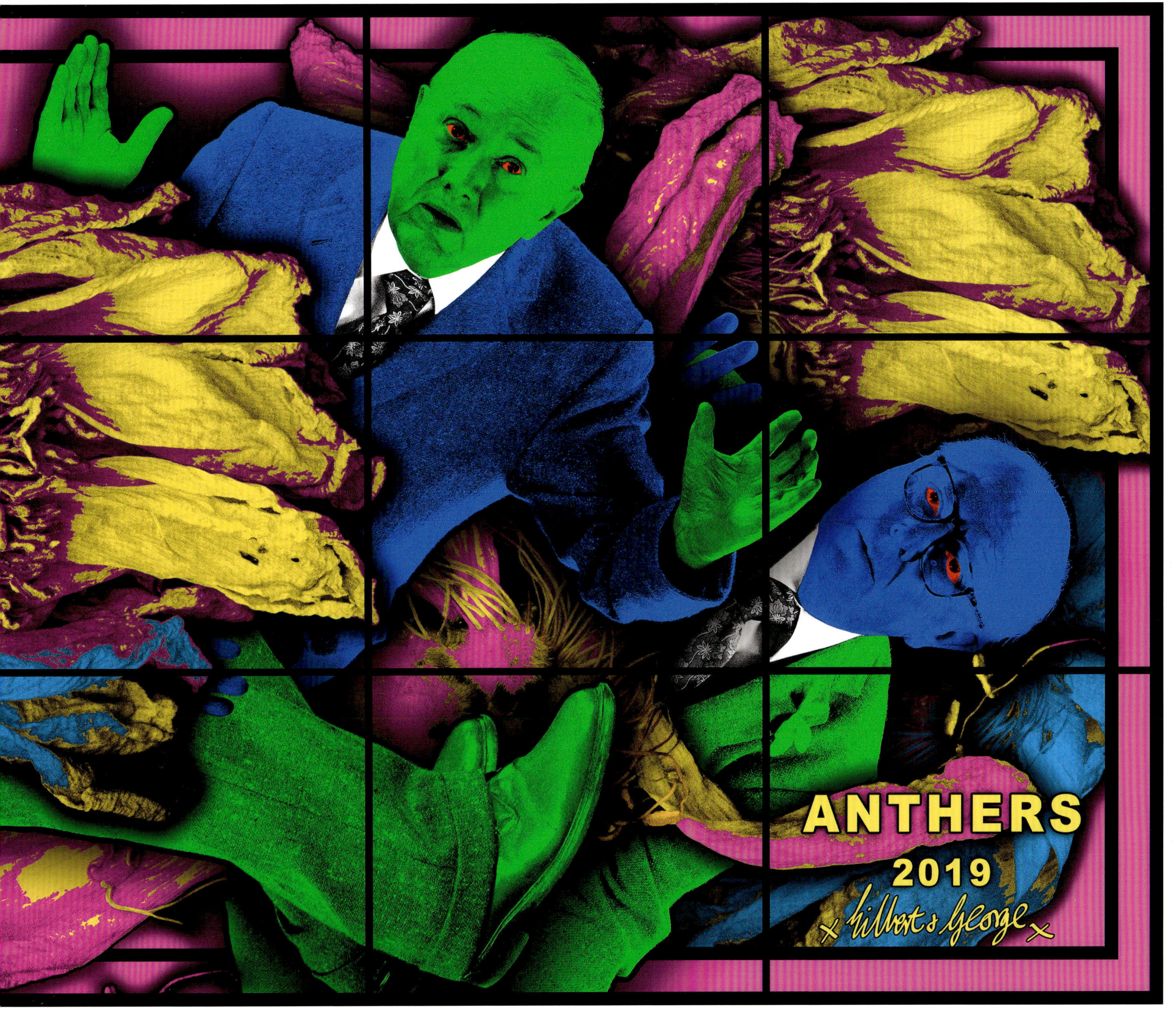
ANTHERS
2019
Gilbert & George

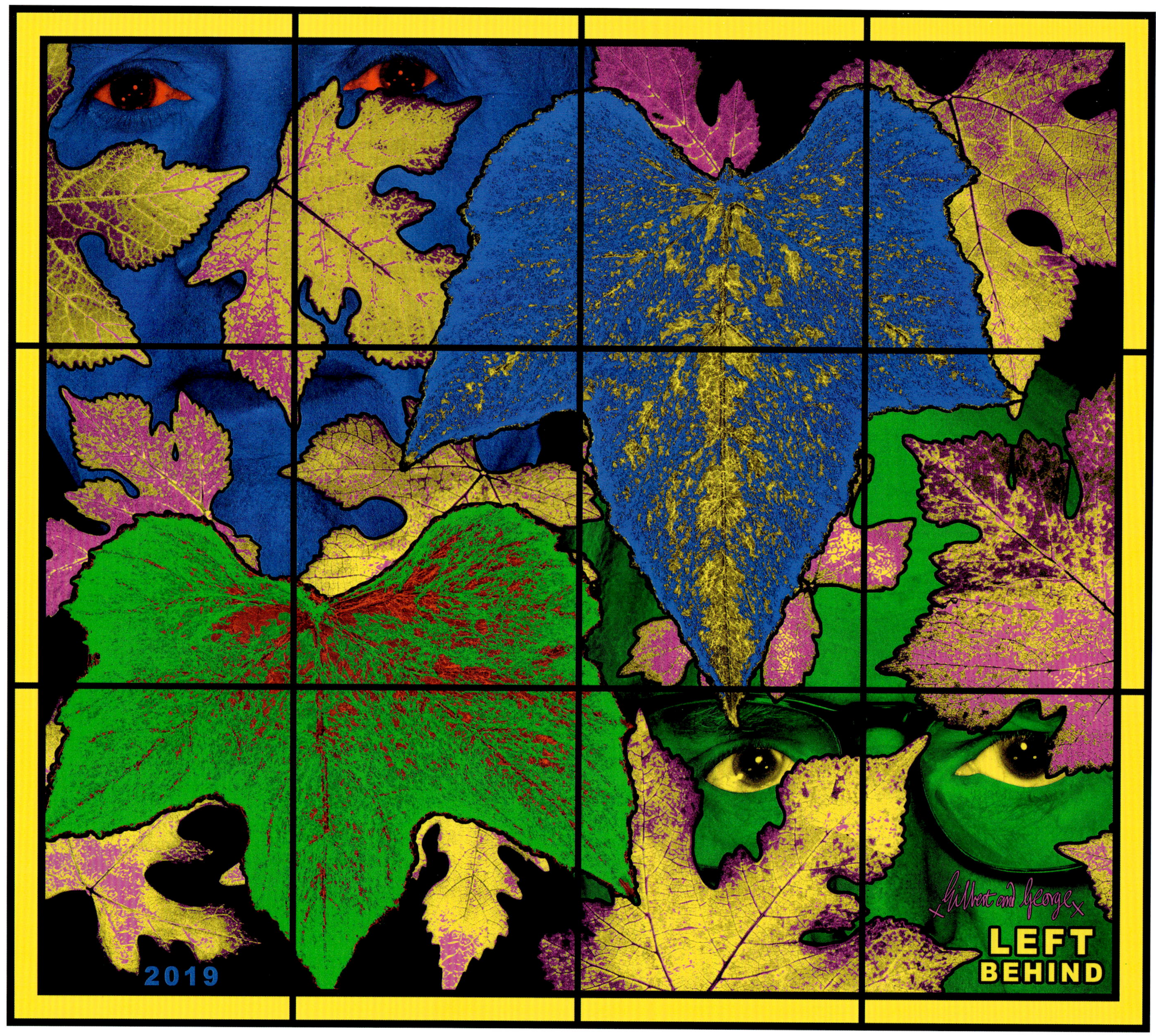

LEFT BEHIND. 2019. 89 x 100 inches (226 x 253 cm)

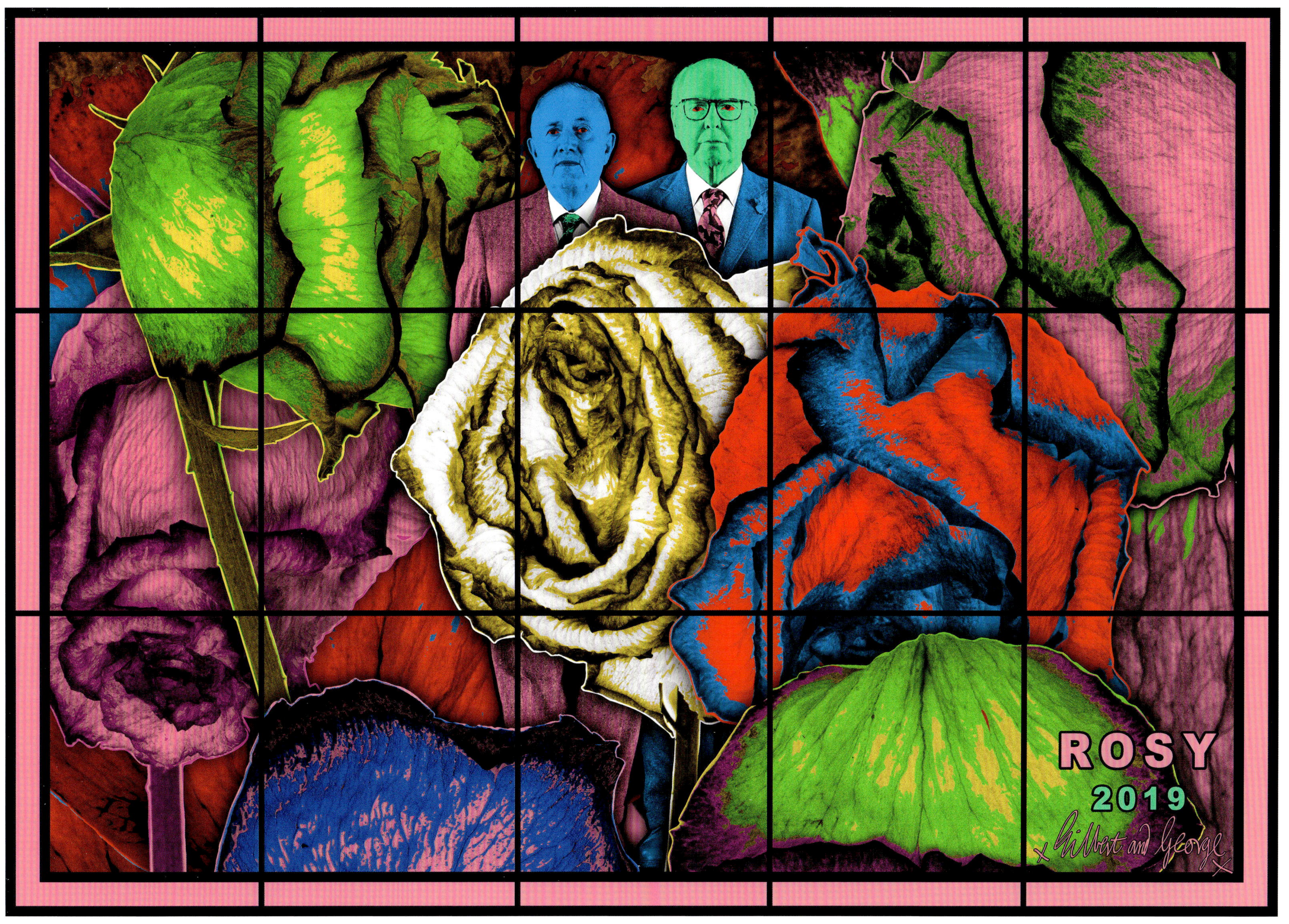

ROSY. 2019. 89 x 125 inches (226 x 316 cm)

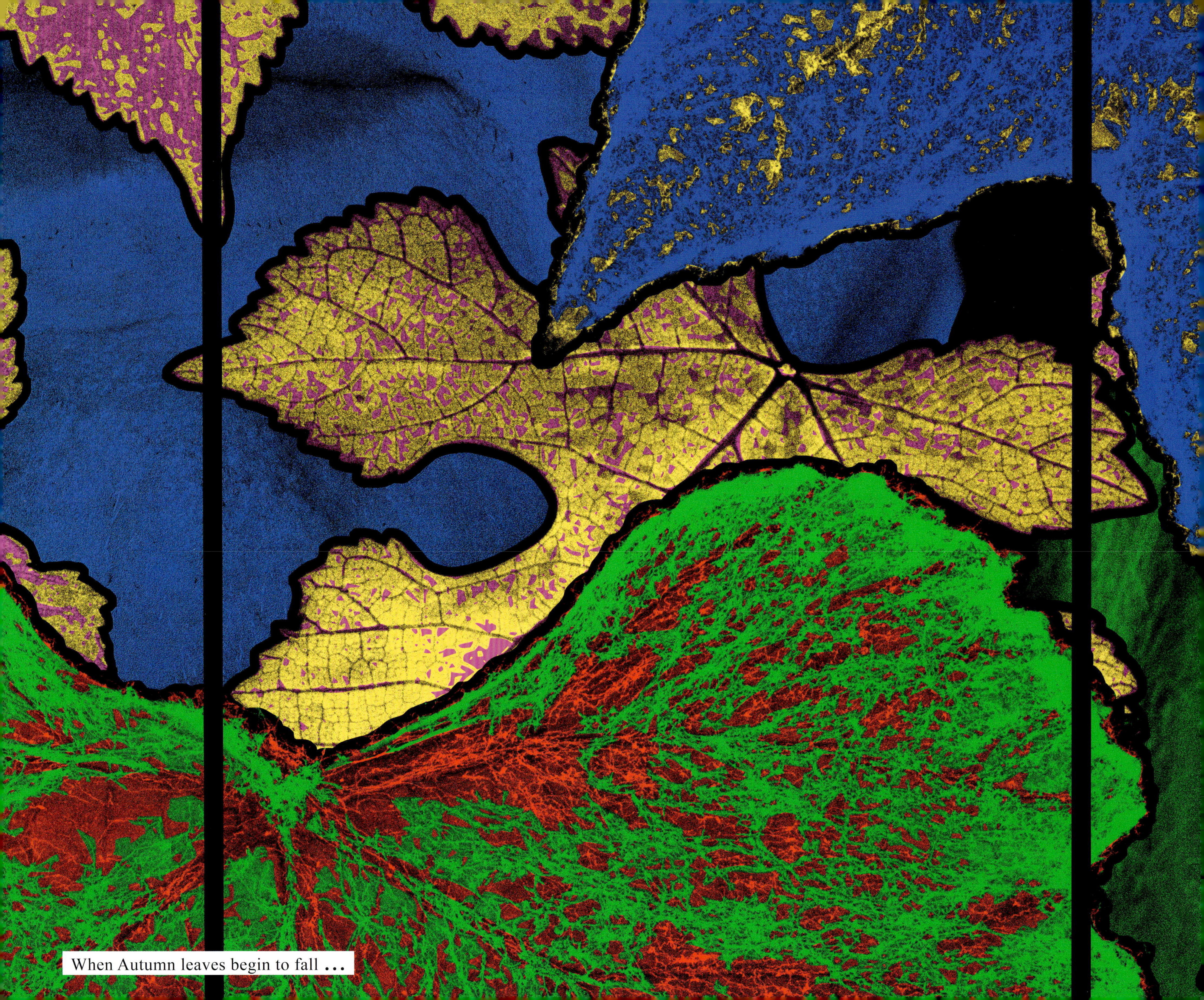
When Autumn leaves begin to fall ...

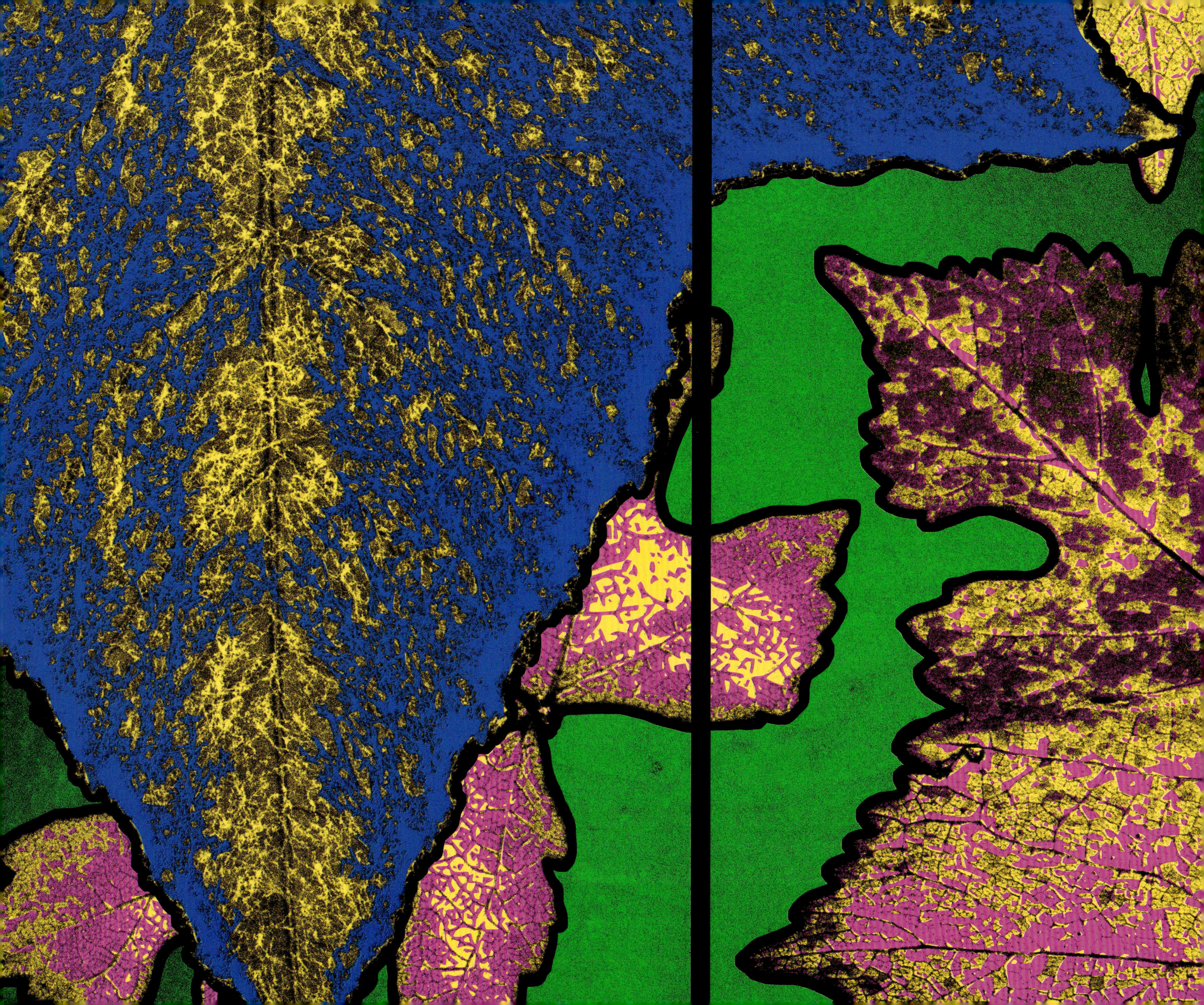

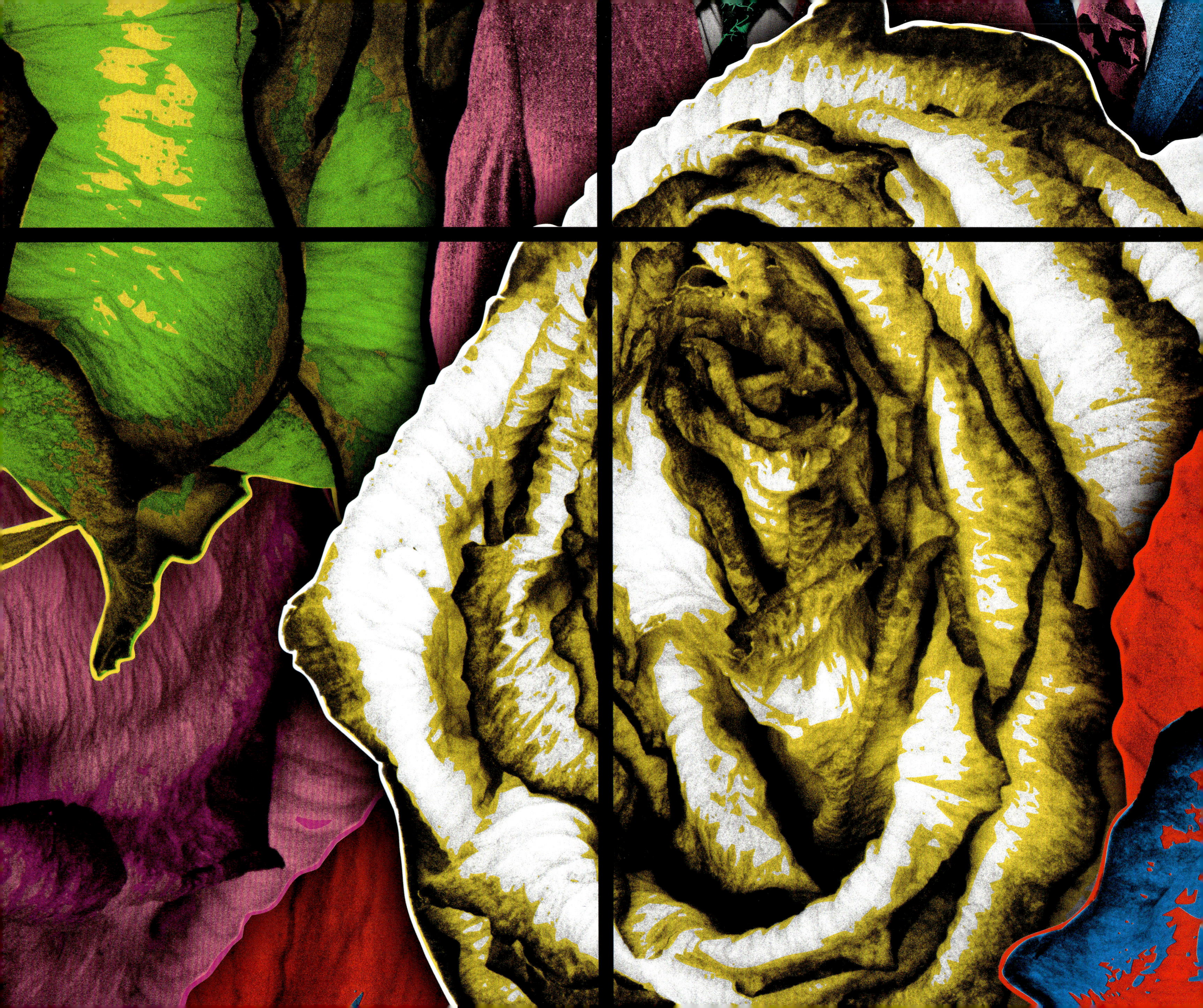

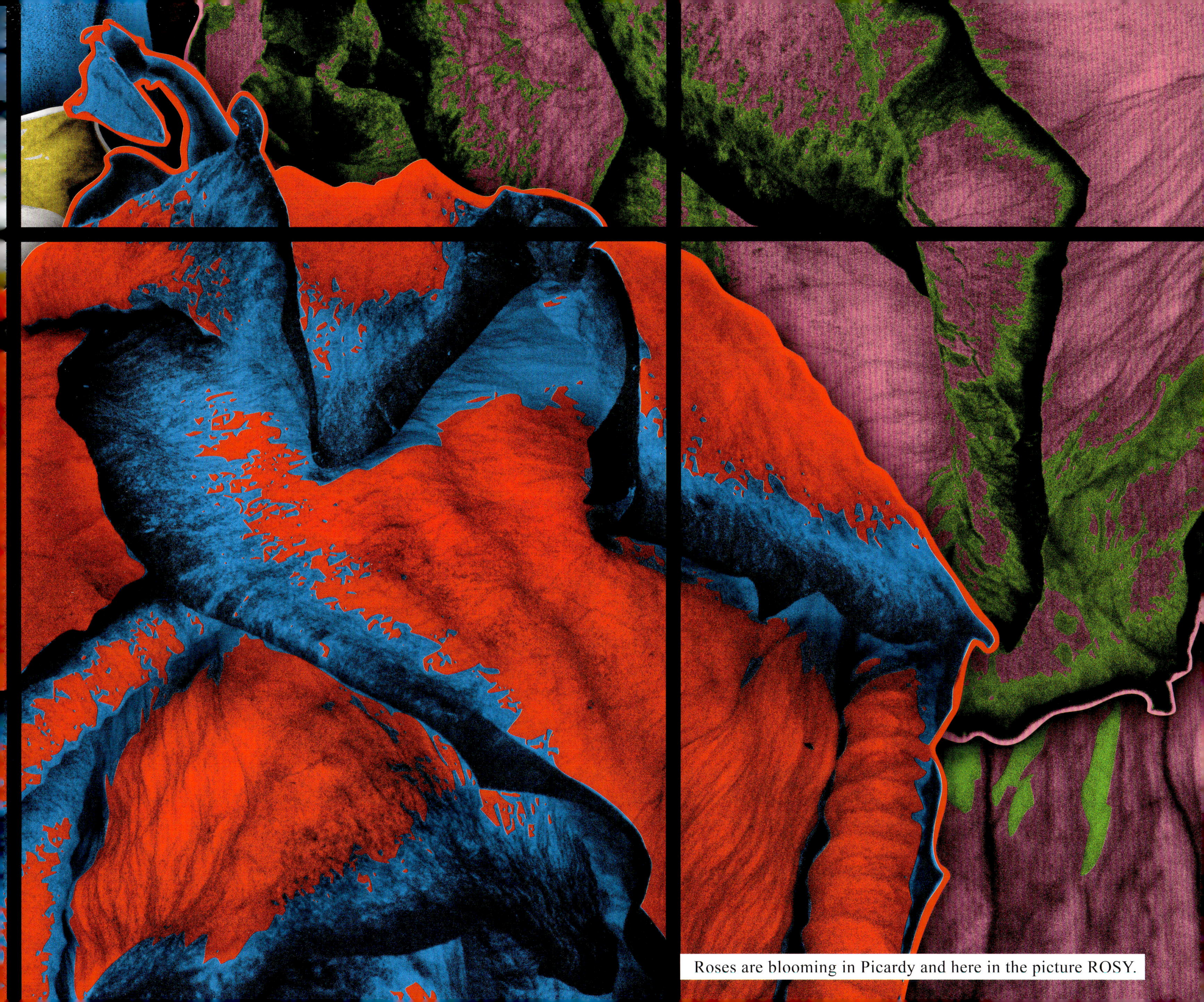

Roses are blooming in Picardy and here in the picture ROSY.

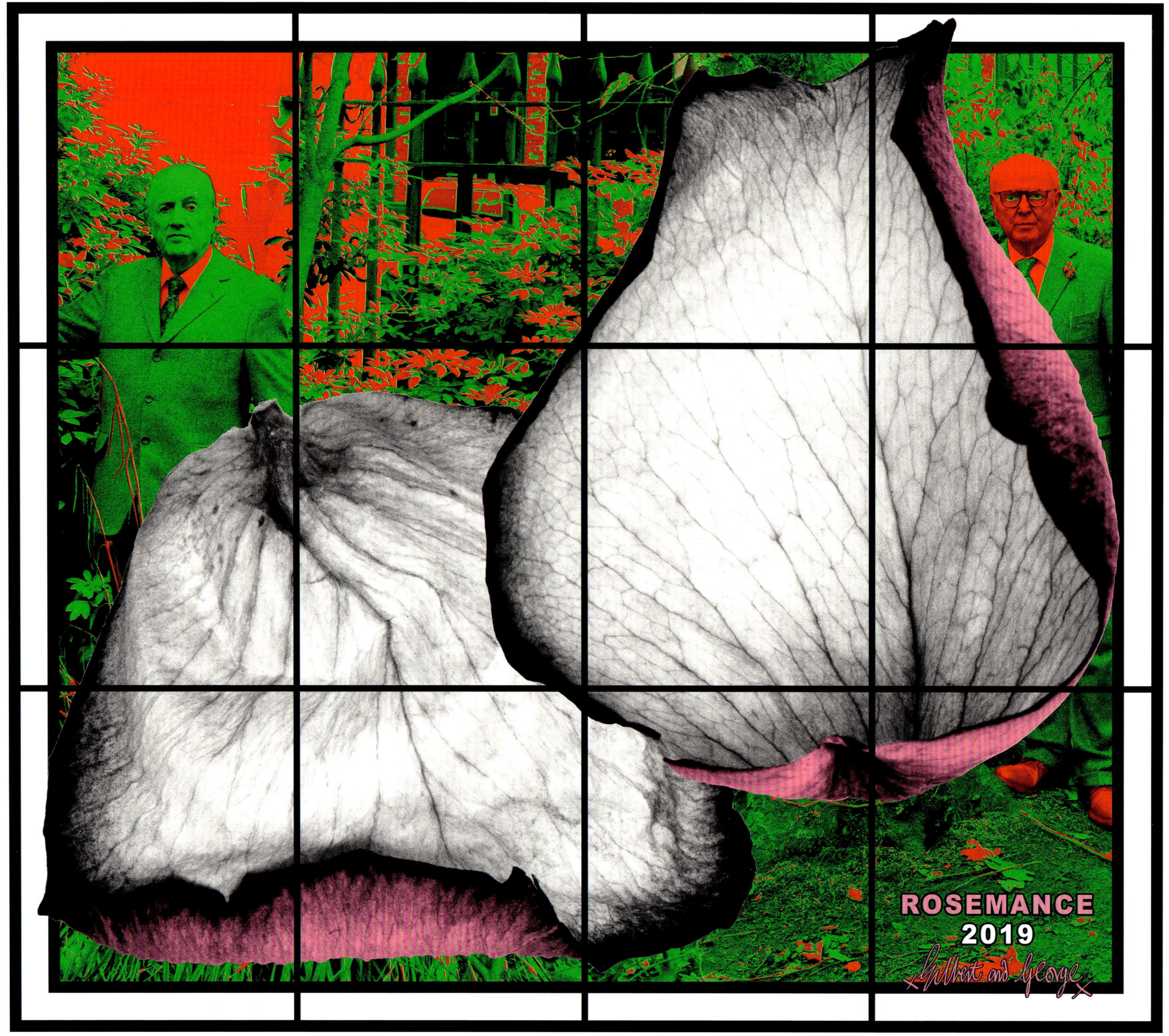

ROSEMANCE. 2019. 89 x 100 inches (226 x 253 cm)

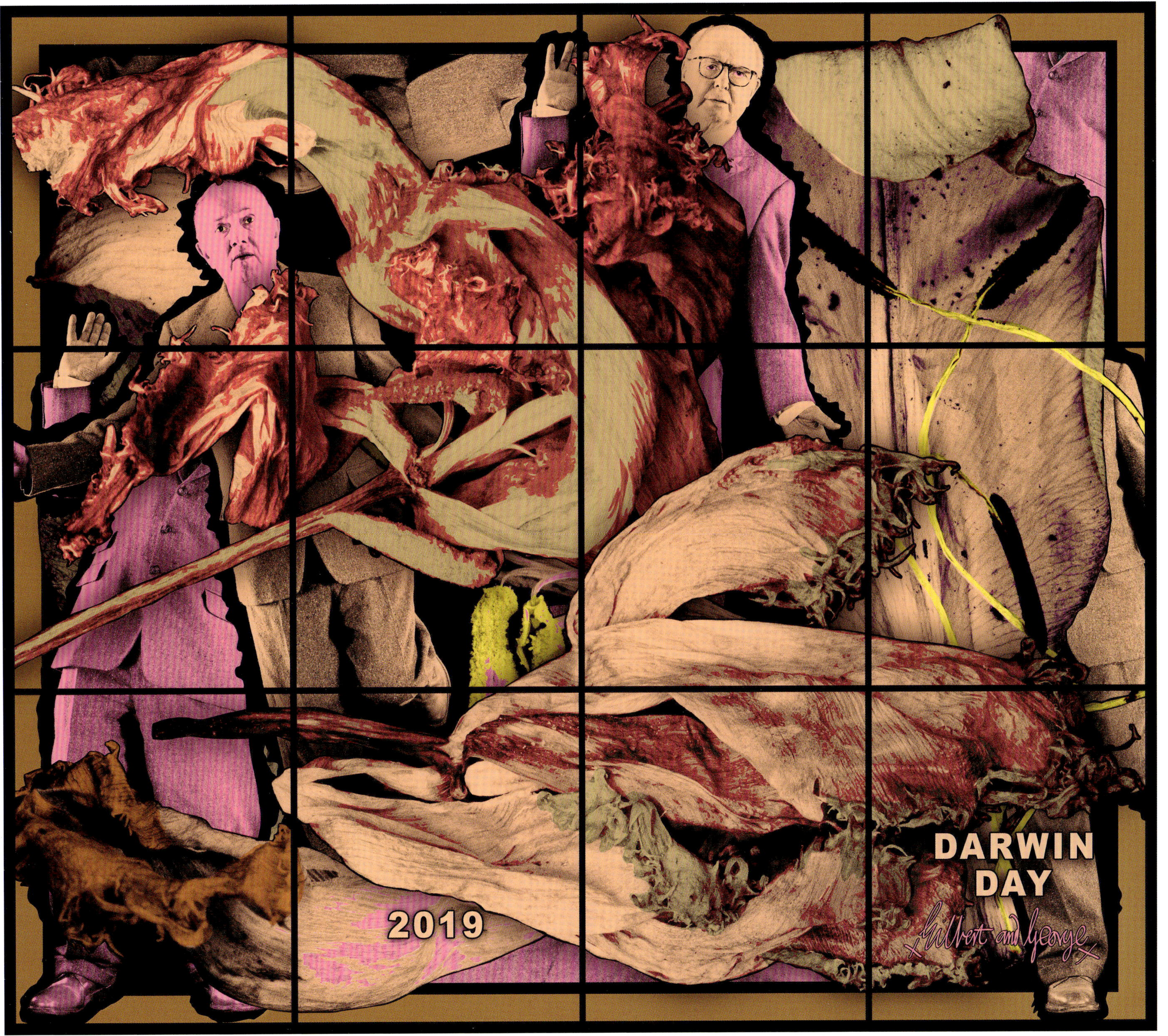

DARWIN DAY. 2019. 89 x 100 inches (226 x 253 cm)

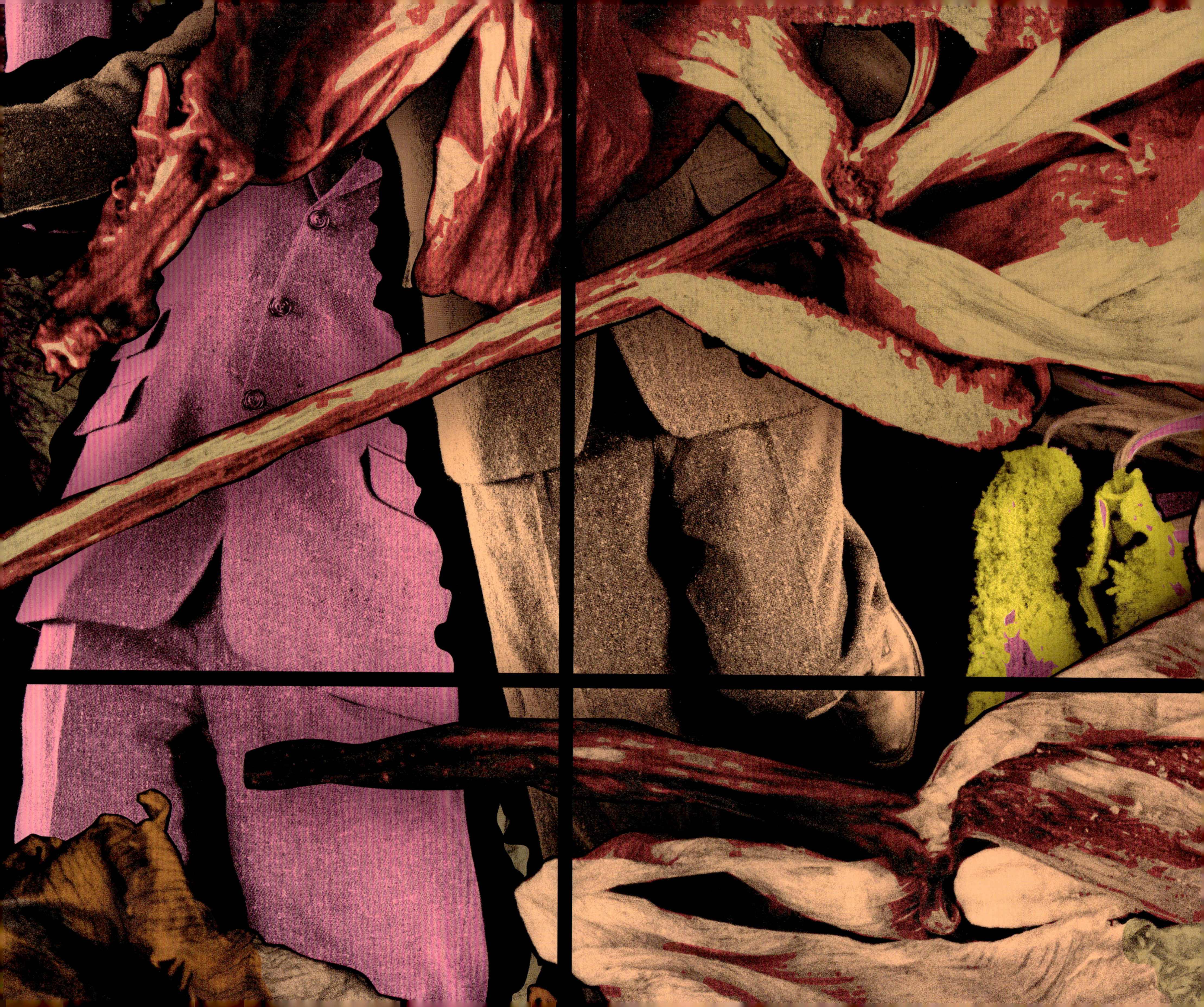

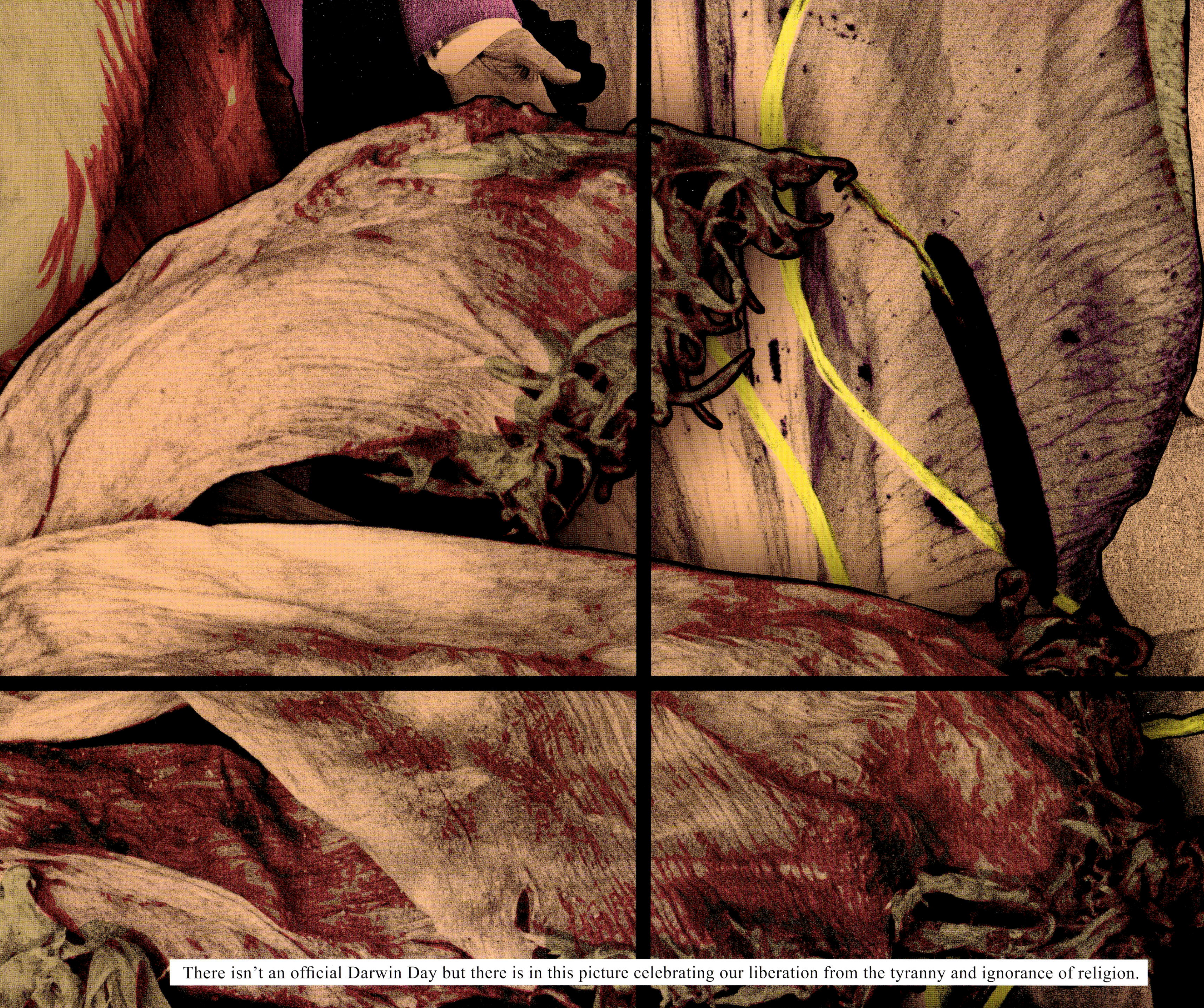
There isn't an official Darwin Day but there is in this picture celebrating our liberation from the tyranny and ignorance of religion.

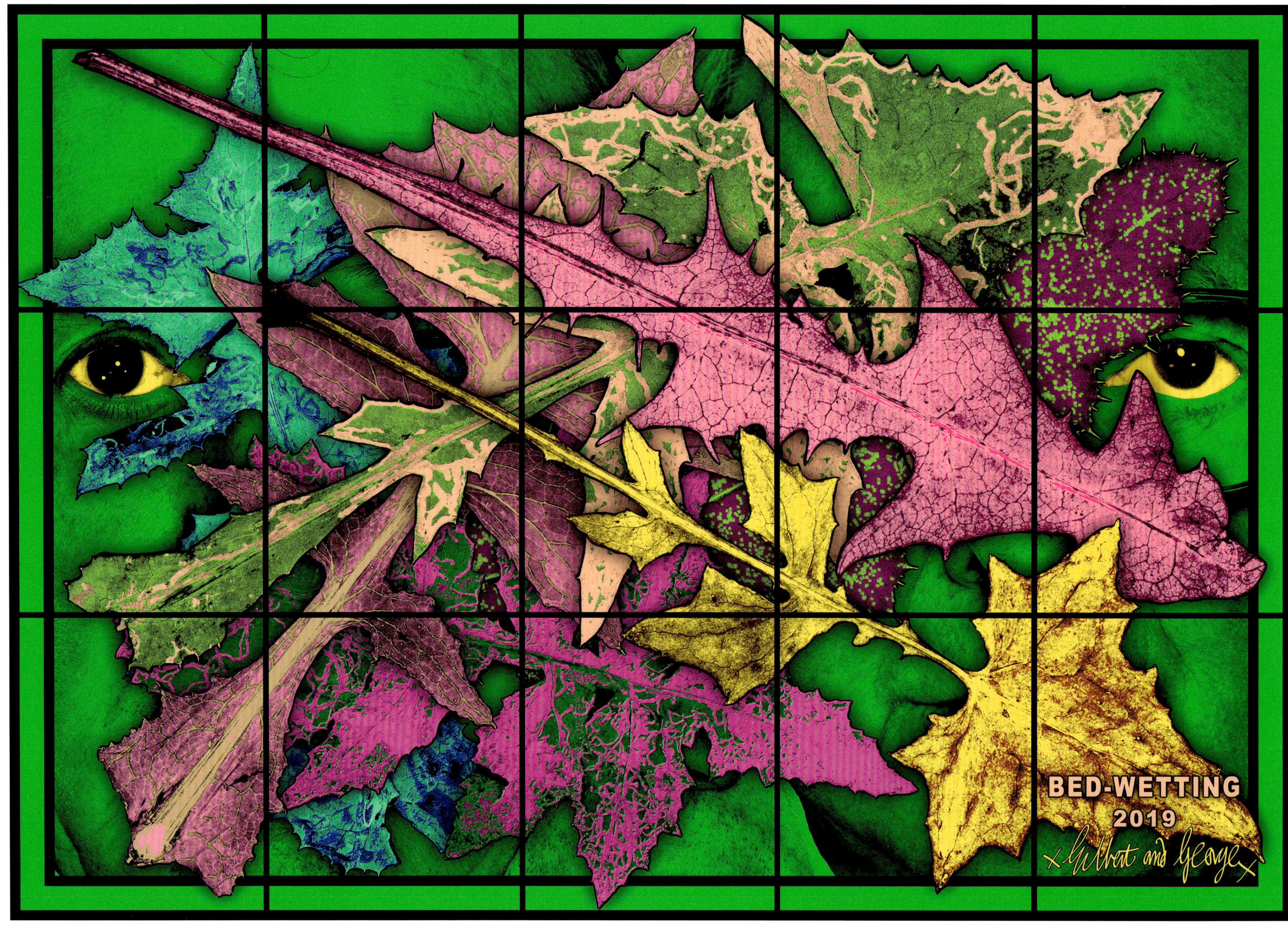

BED-WETTING. 2019. 89 x 125 inches (226 x 316 cm)

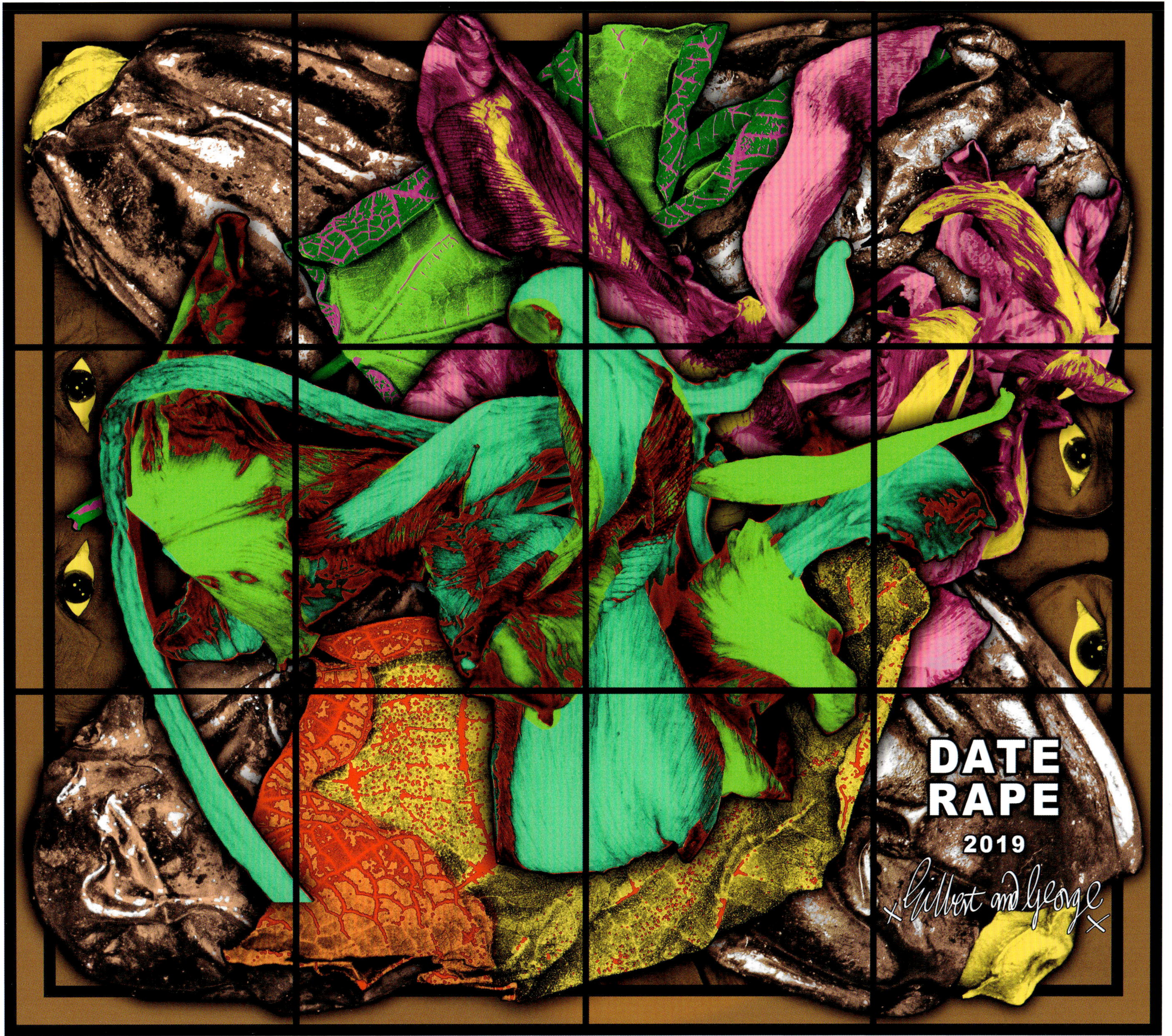

DATE RAPE. 2019. 89 x 100 inches (226 x 253 cm)

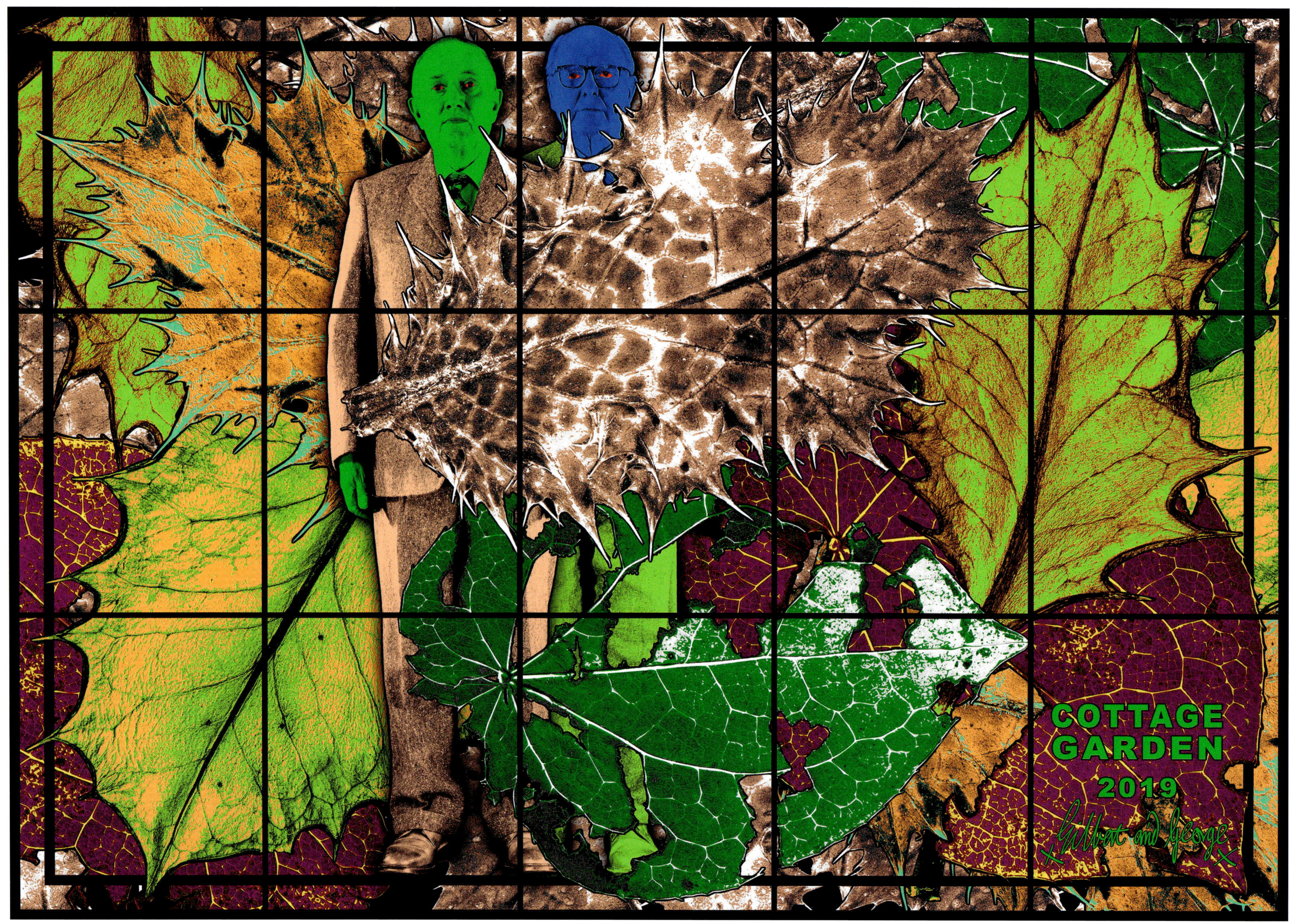

COTTAGE GARDEN. 2019. 89 x 125 inches (226 x 316 cm)

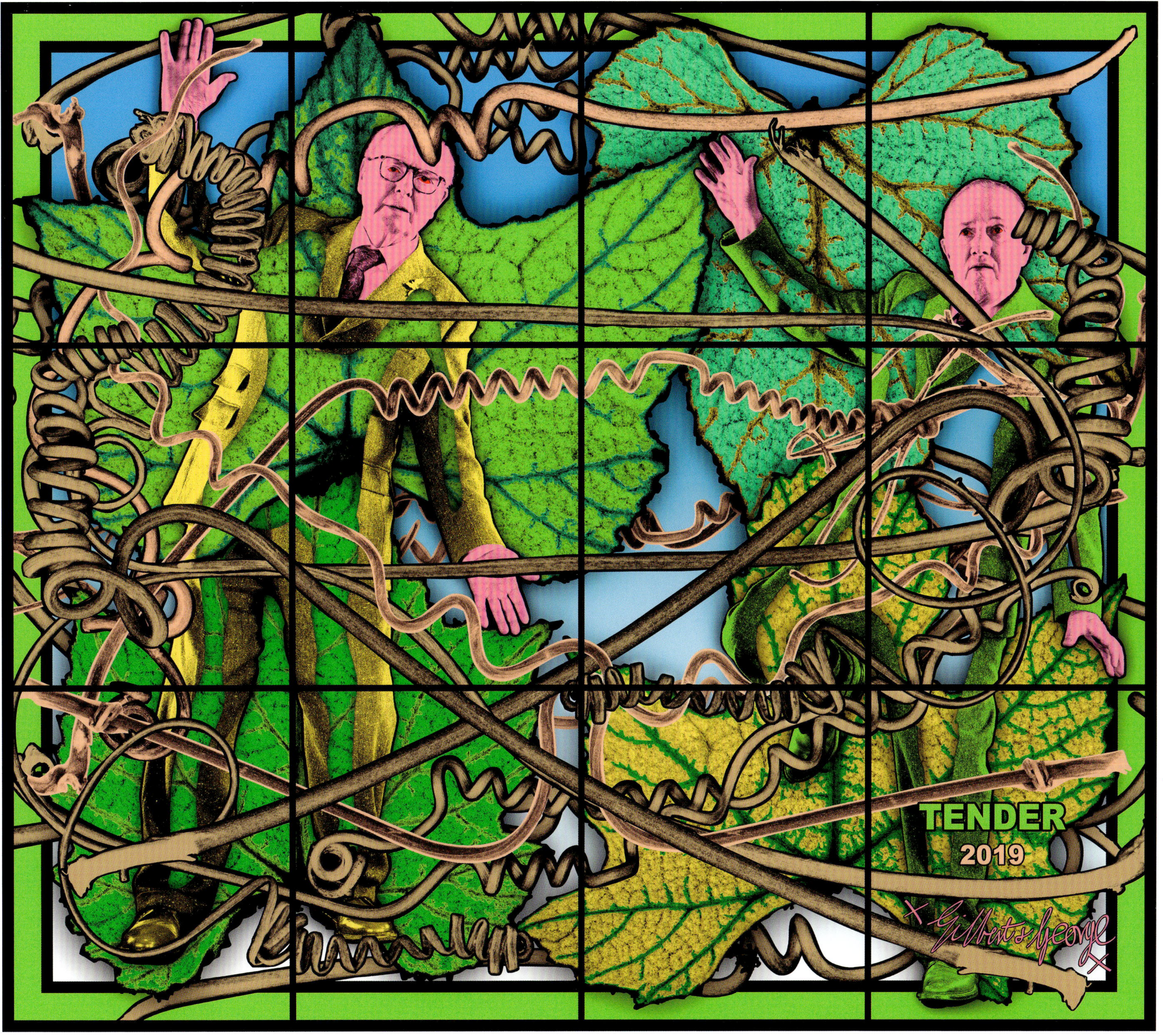

TENDER. 2019. 89 x 100 inches (226 x 253 cm)

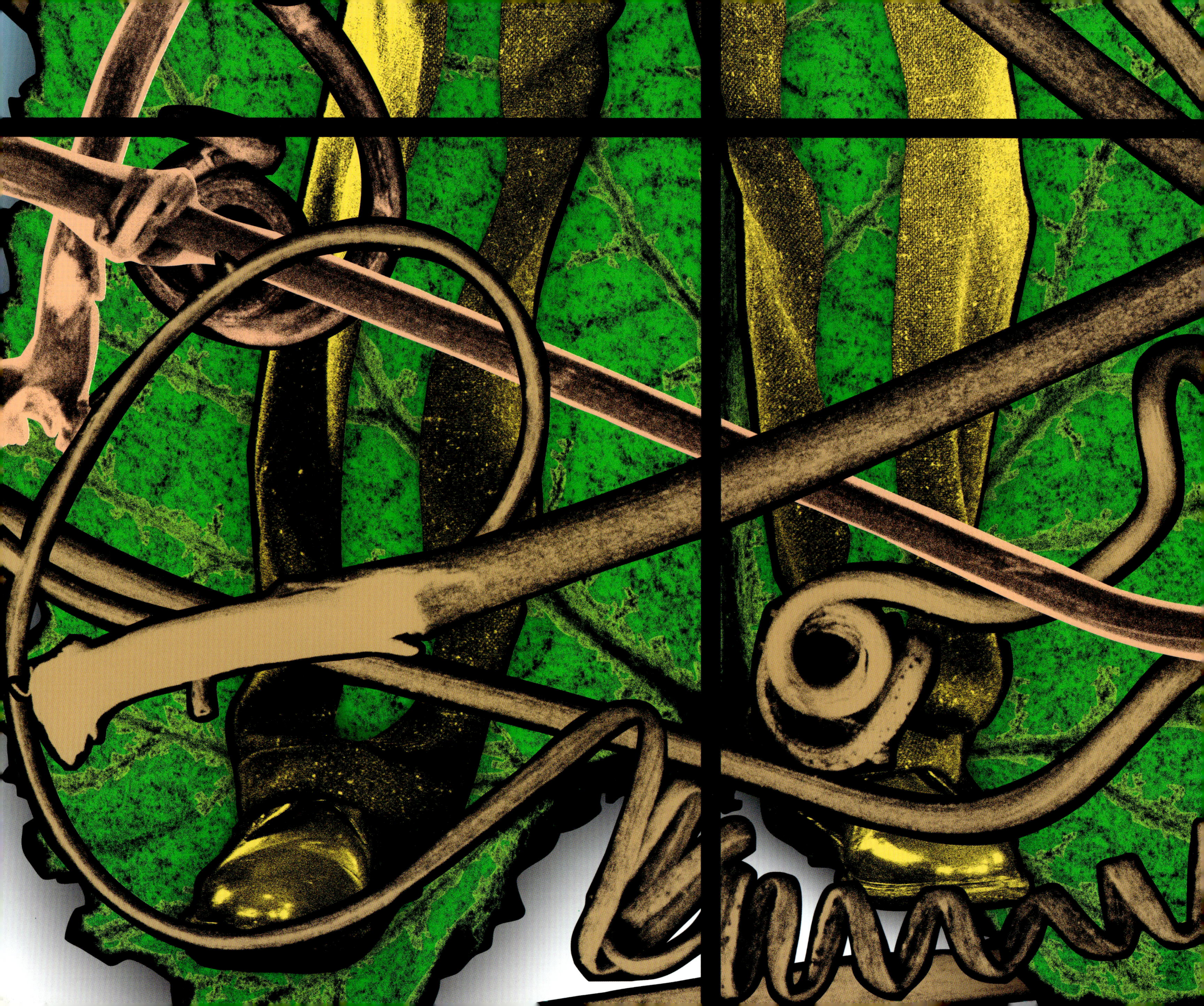

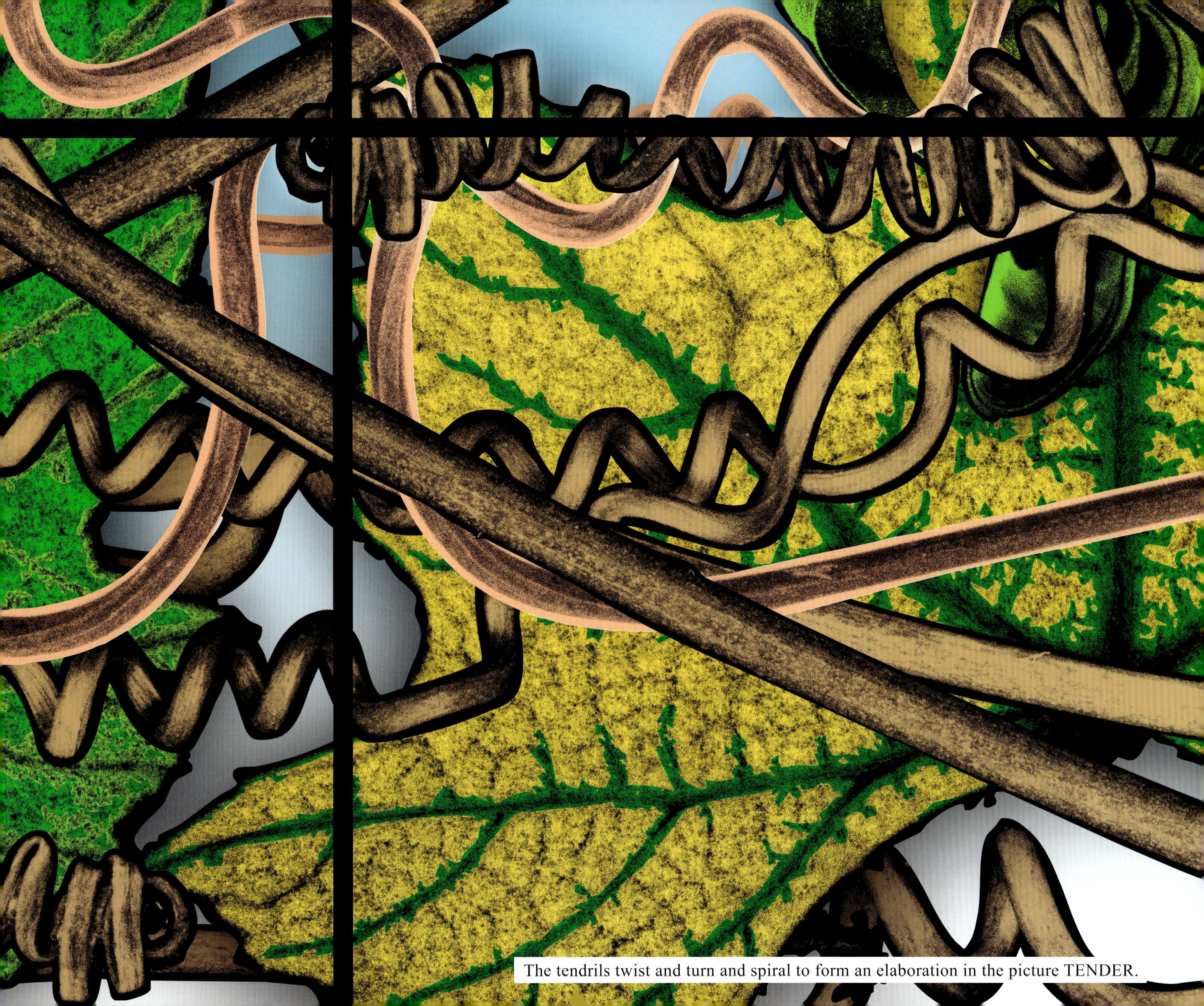

The tendrils twist and turn and spiral to form an elaboration in the picture TENDER.

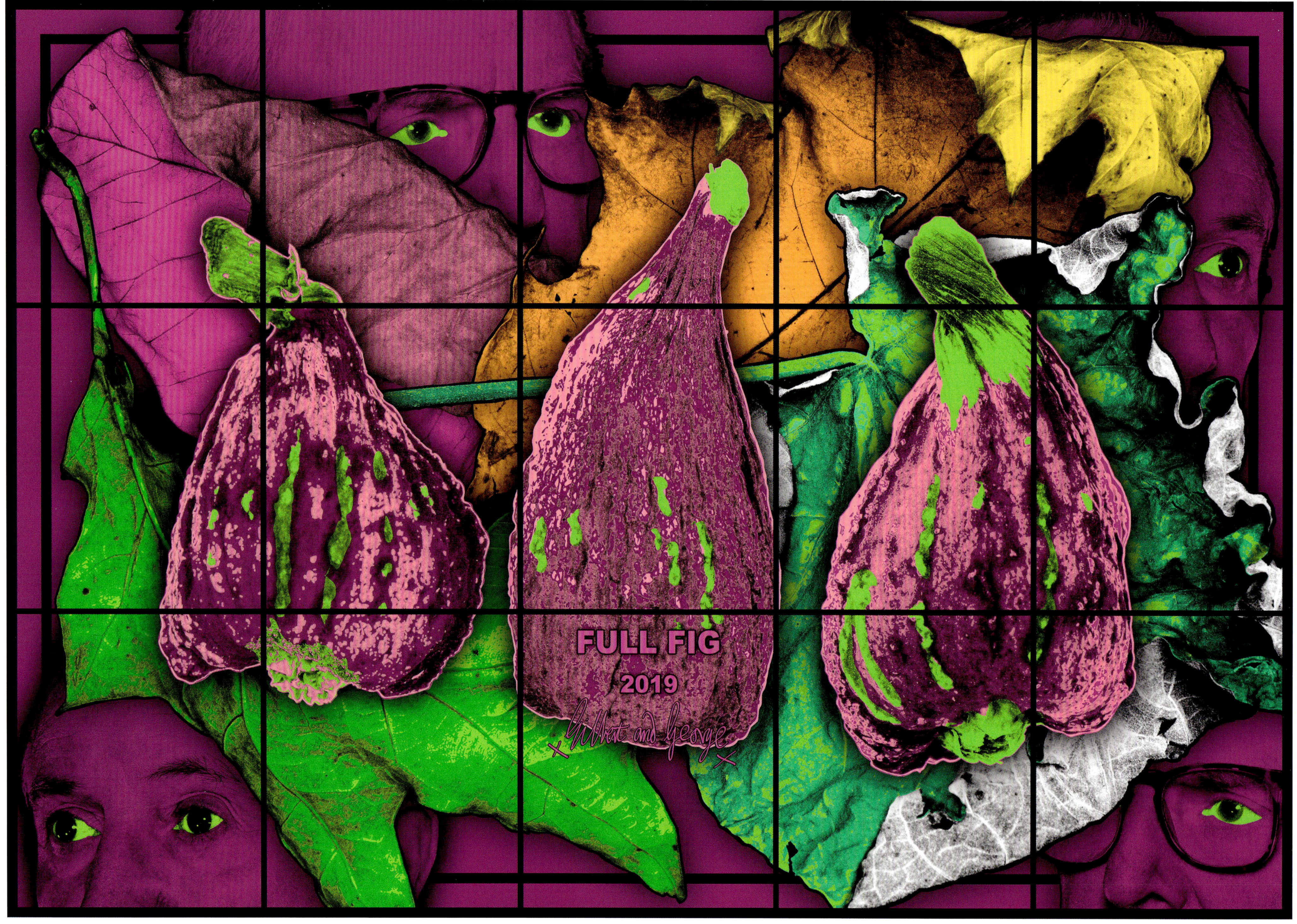

FULL FIG. 2019. 89 x 125 inches (226 x 316 cm)

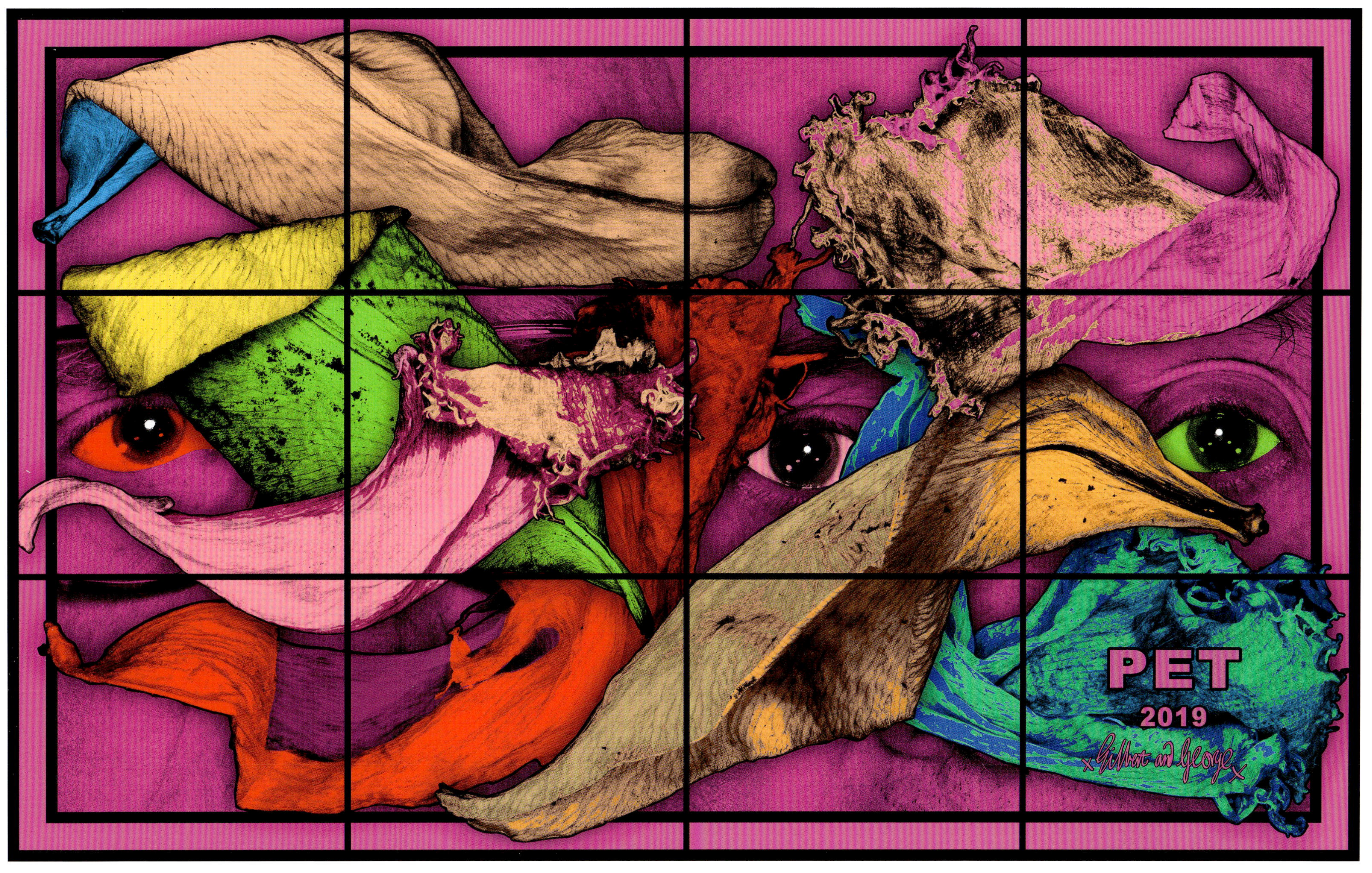

PET. 2019. 75 x 119 inches (190 x 301 cm)

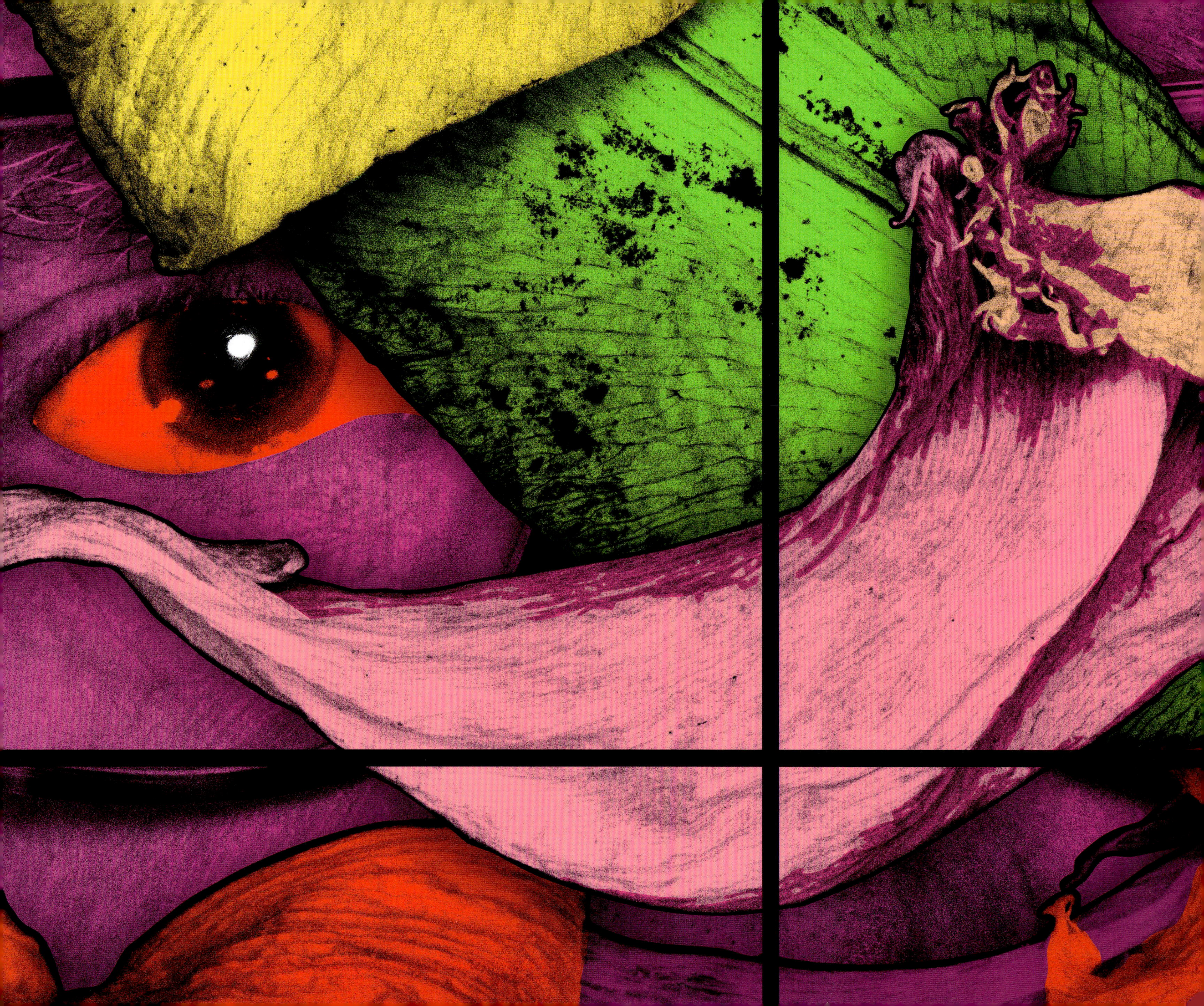

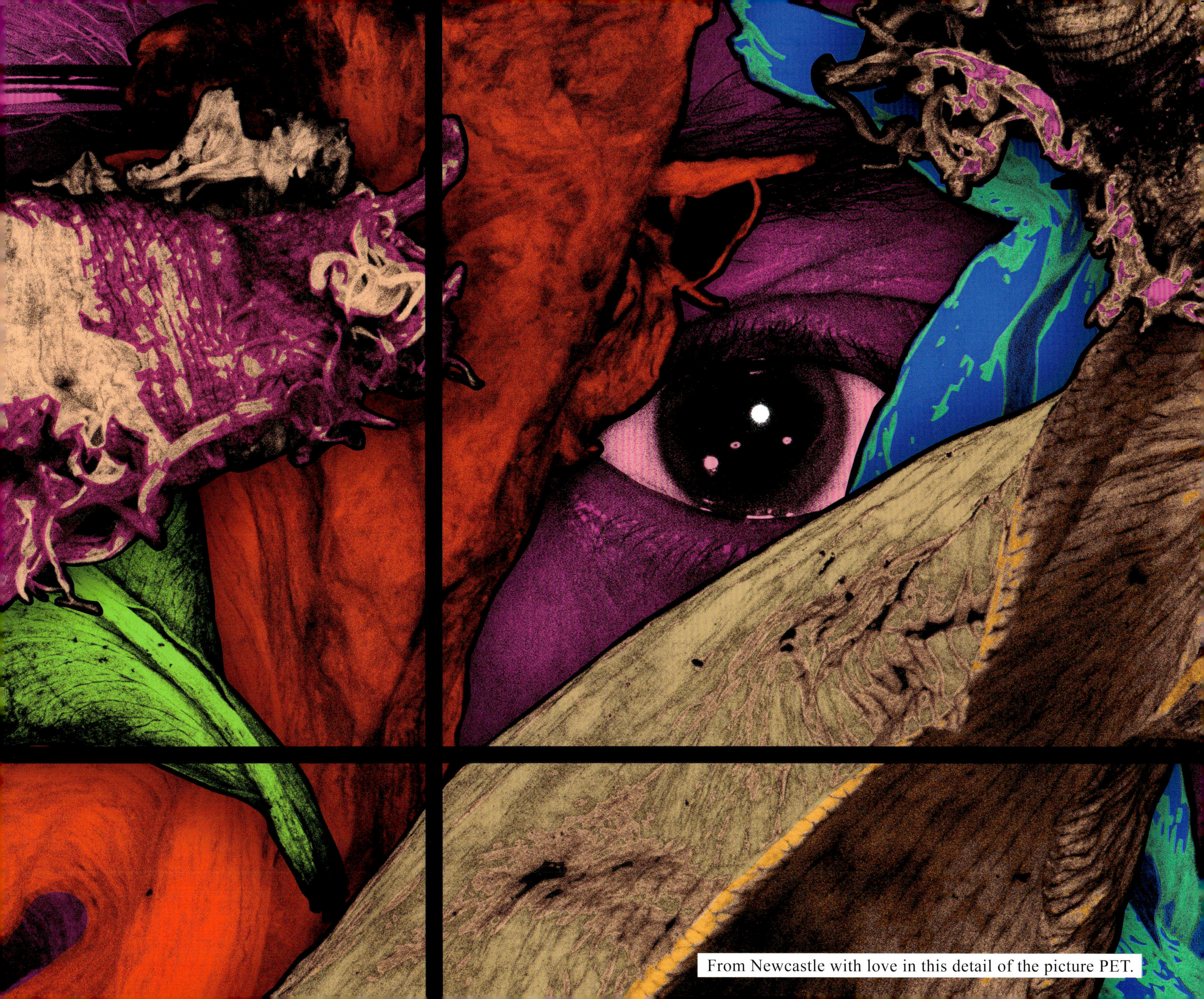

From Newcastle with love in this detail of the picture PET.

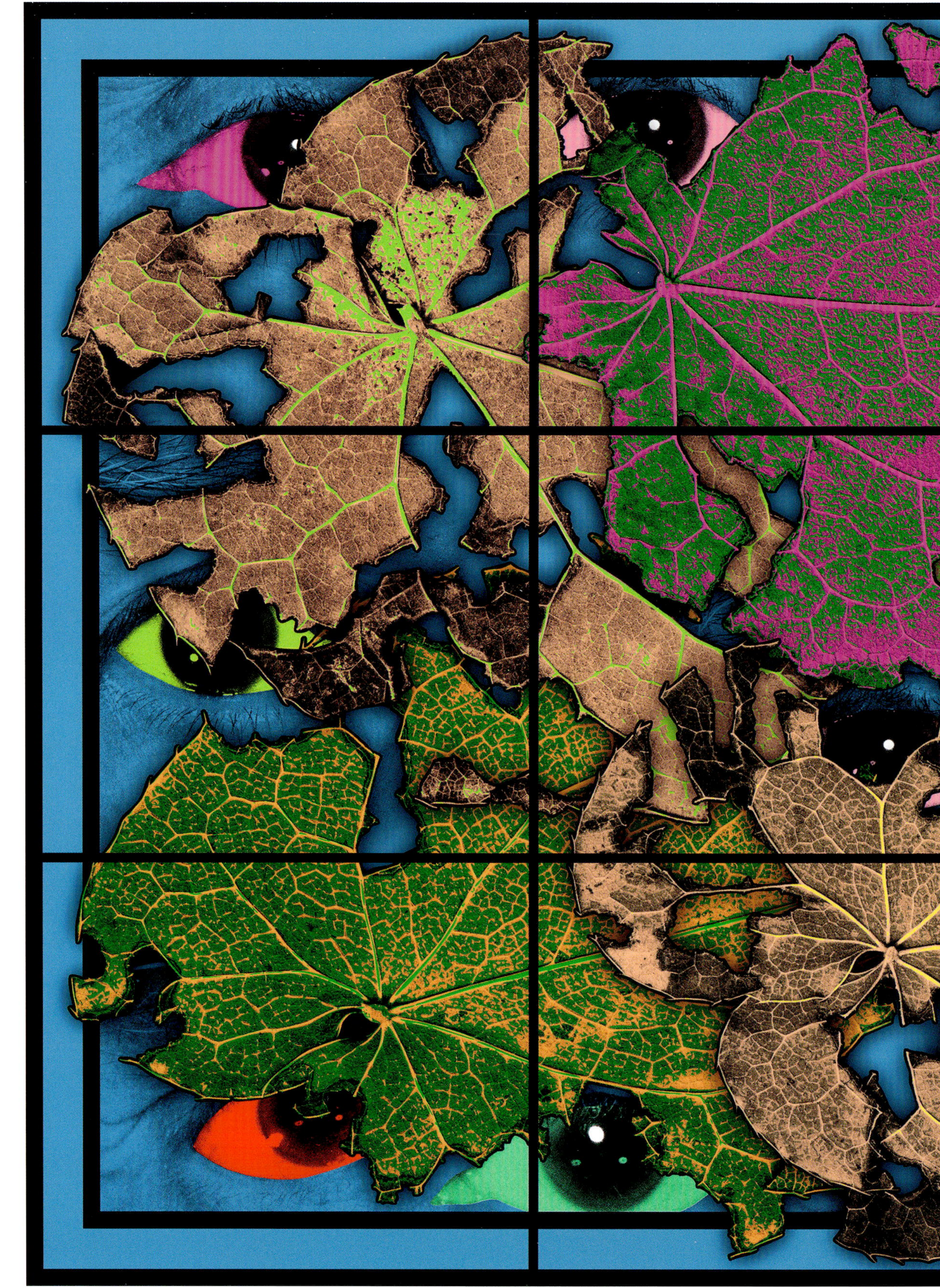

EATEN MESS. 2019. 75 x 119 inches (190 x 301 cm)

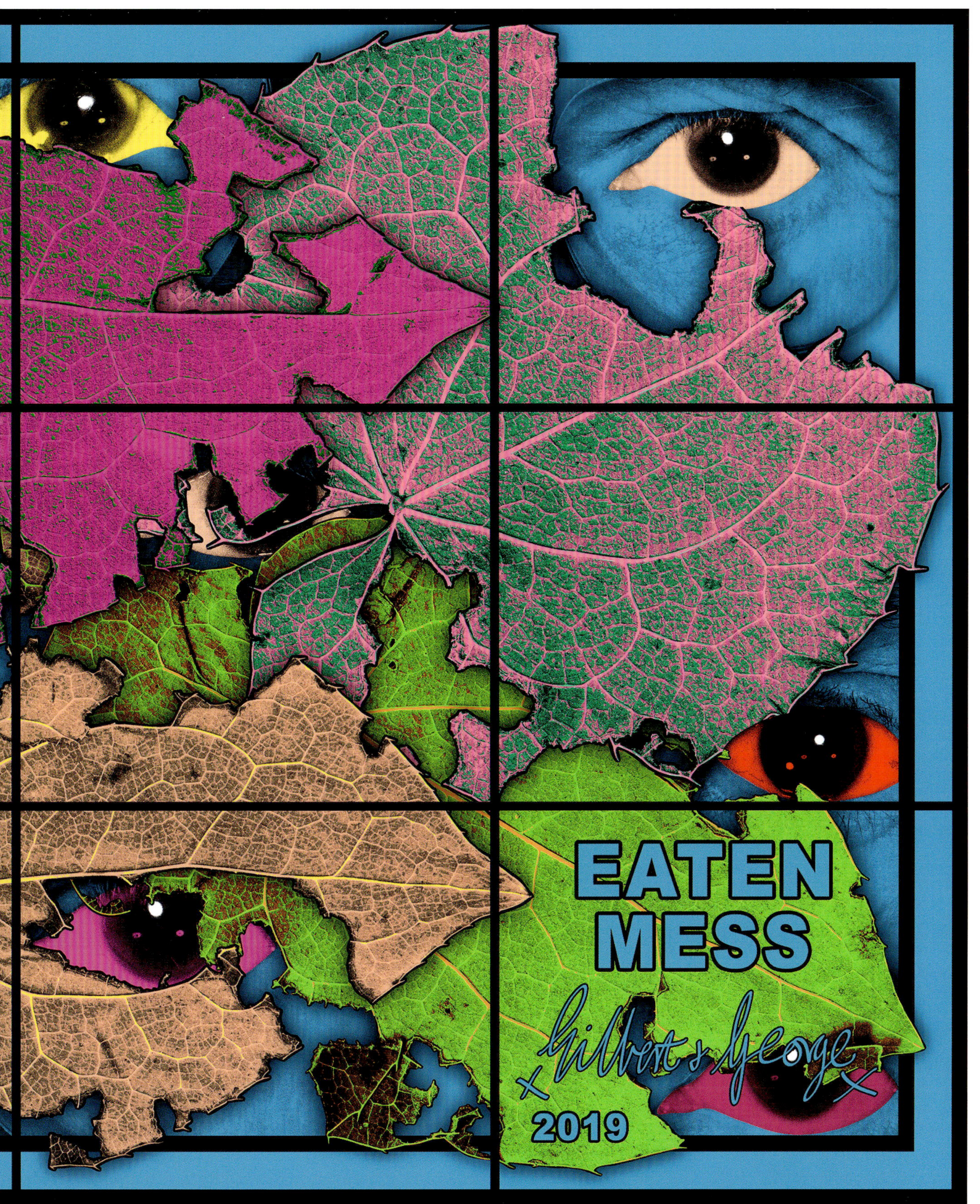
EATEN
MESS
Gilbert & George
2019

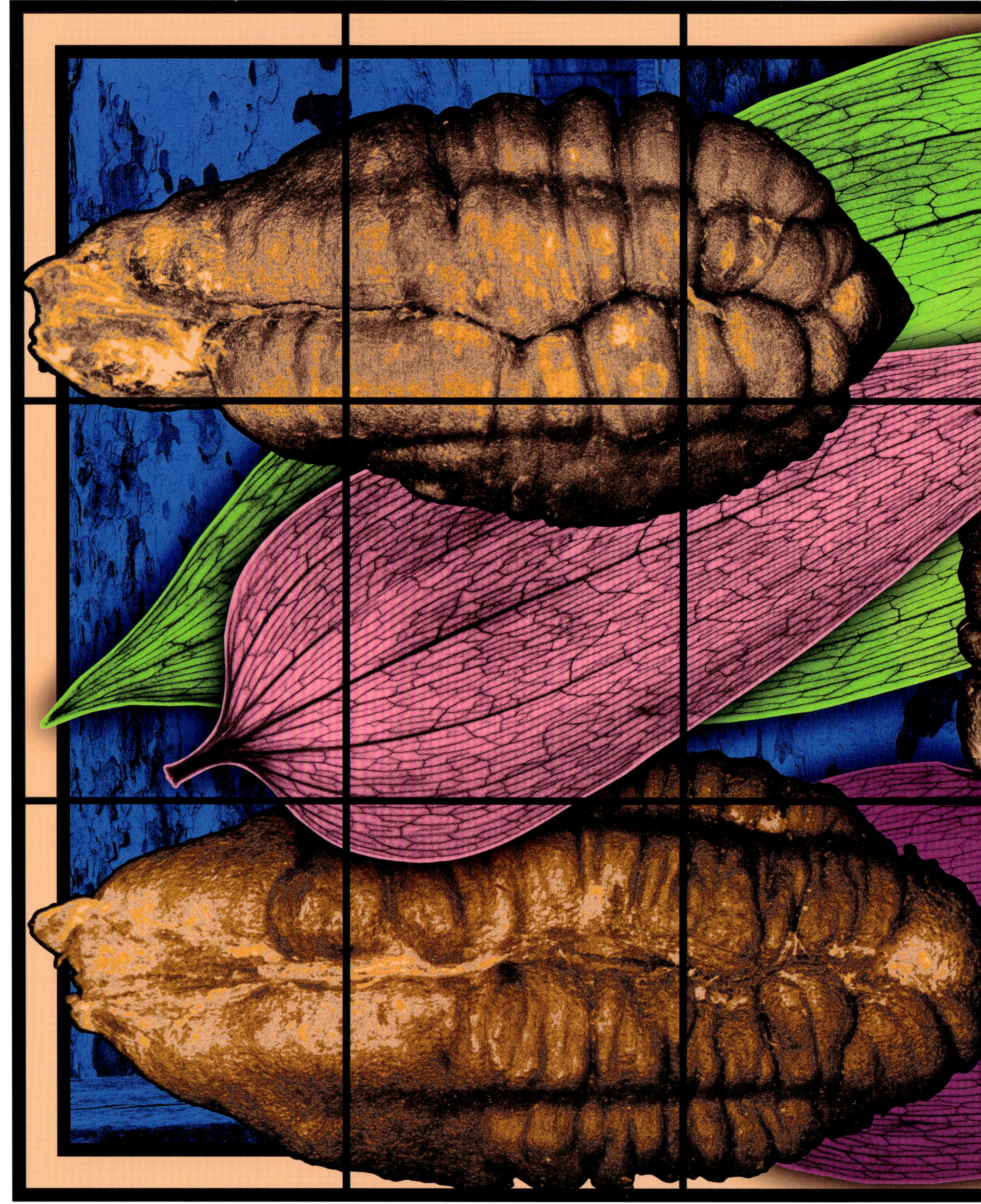

DATE STONES. 2019.
89 x 174 inches (226 x 442 cm)

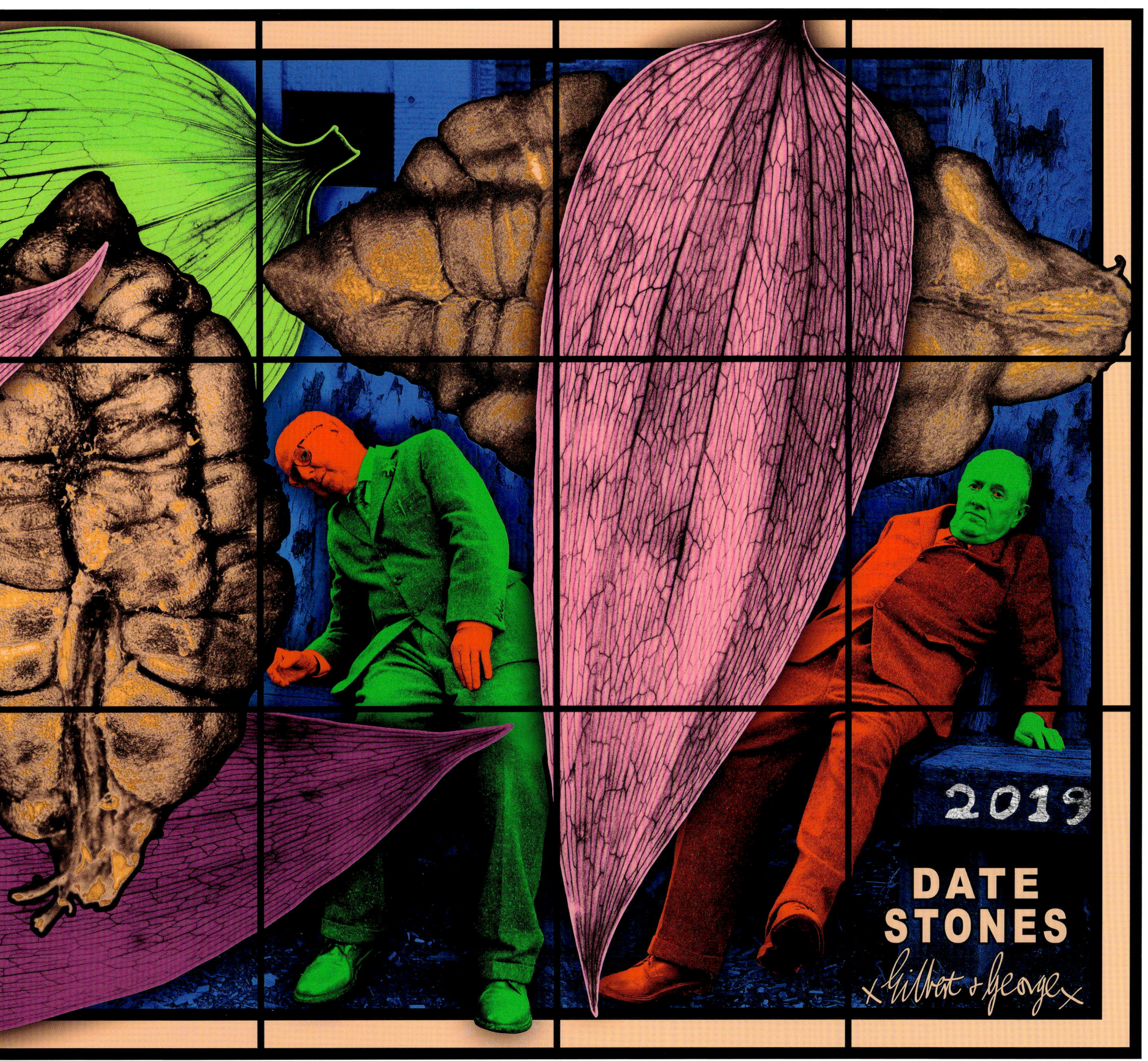
2019
DATE
STONES
Gilbert & George

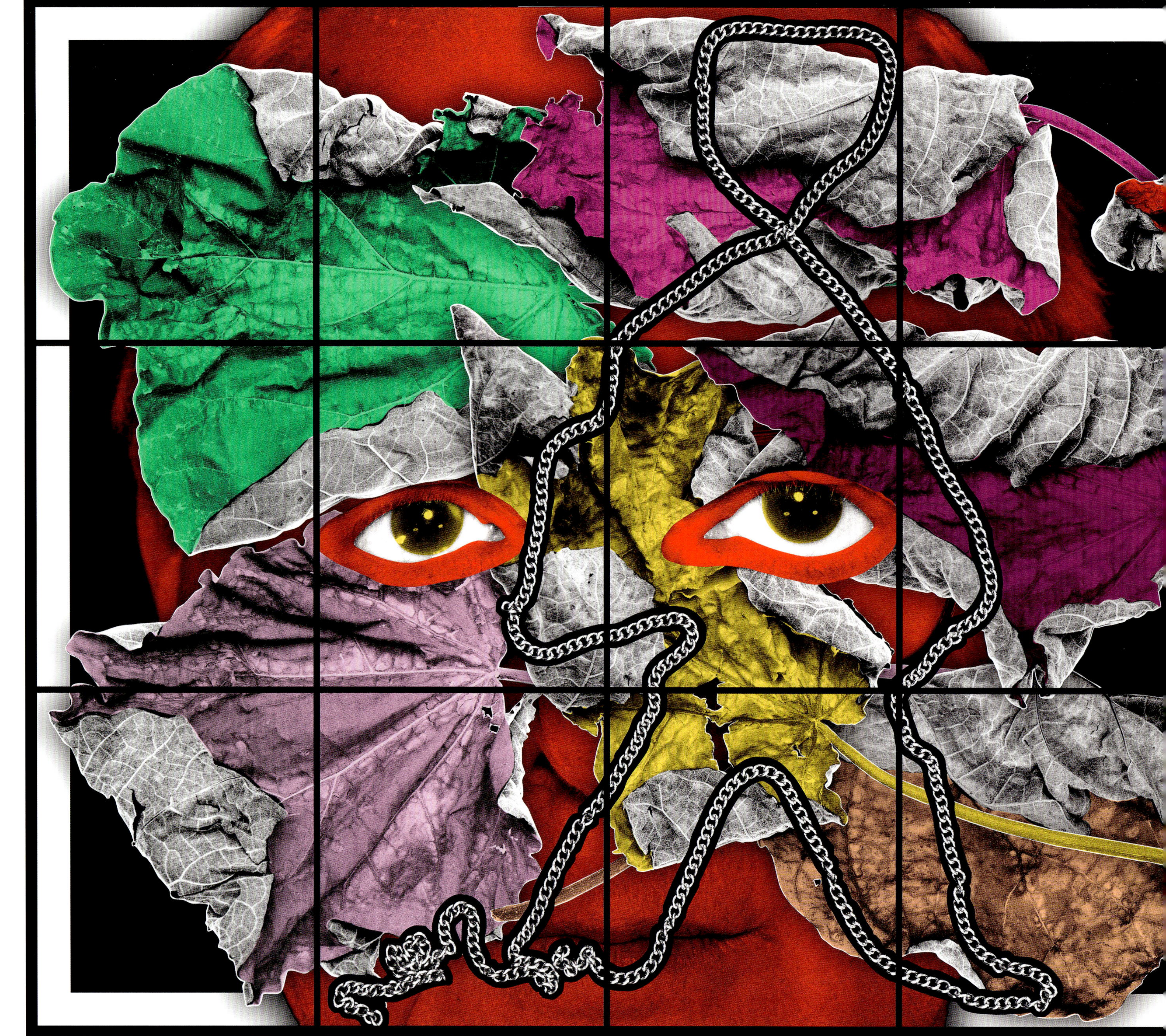

CHAIN BRAIN.
2019.
89 x 199 inches
(226 x 505 cm)

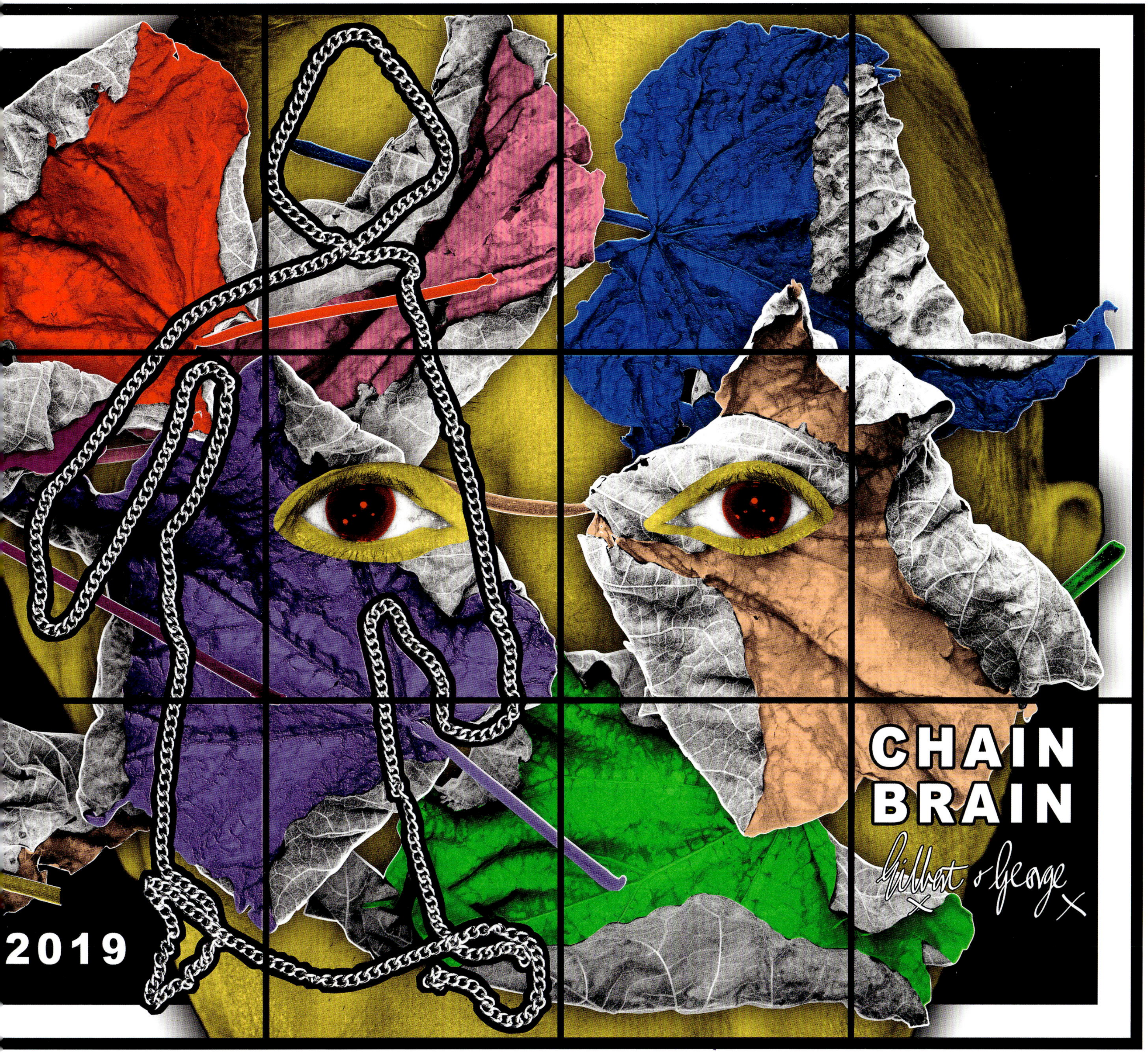
CHAIN
BRAIN
Gilbert & George
2019

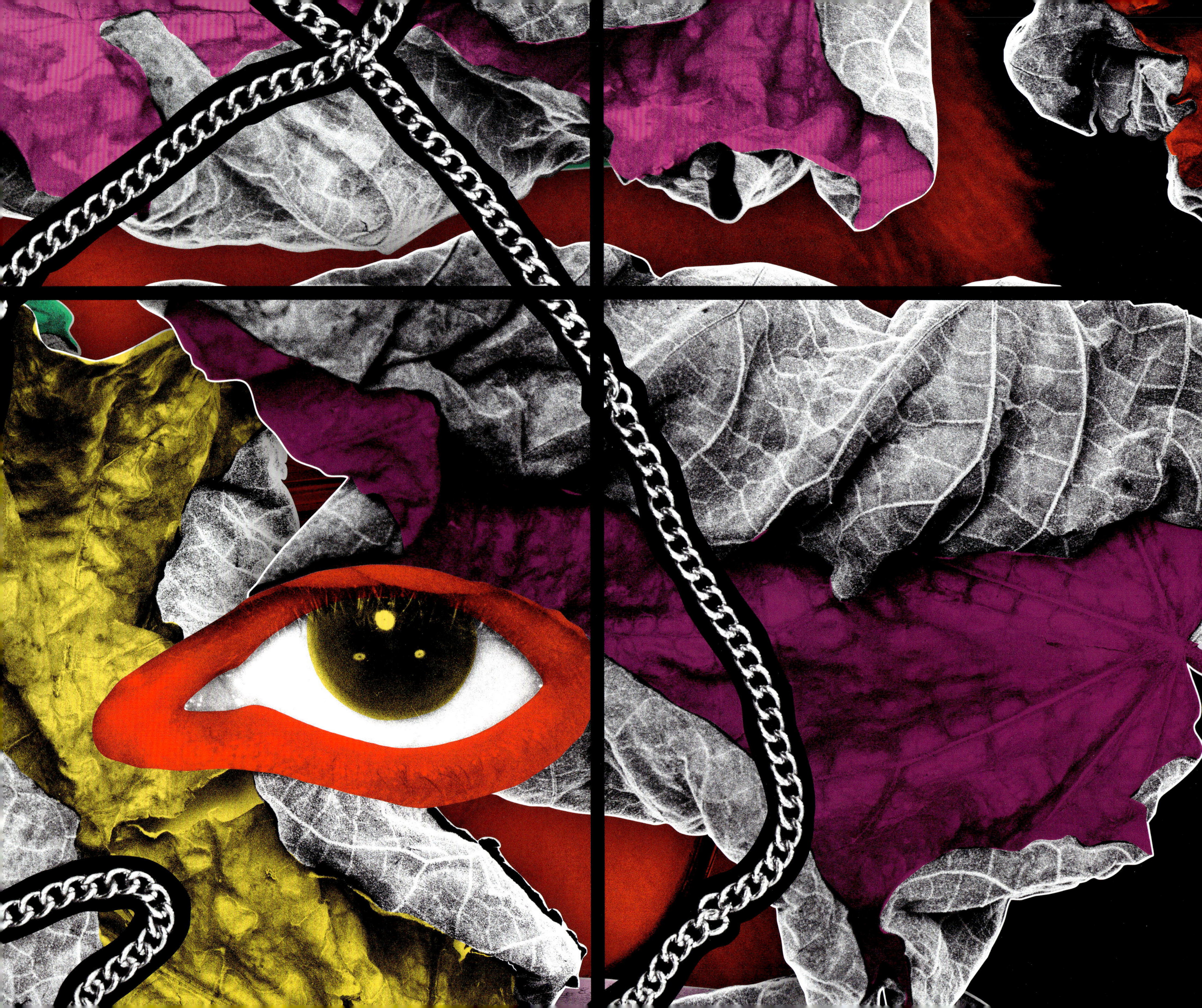

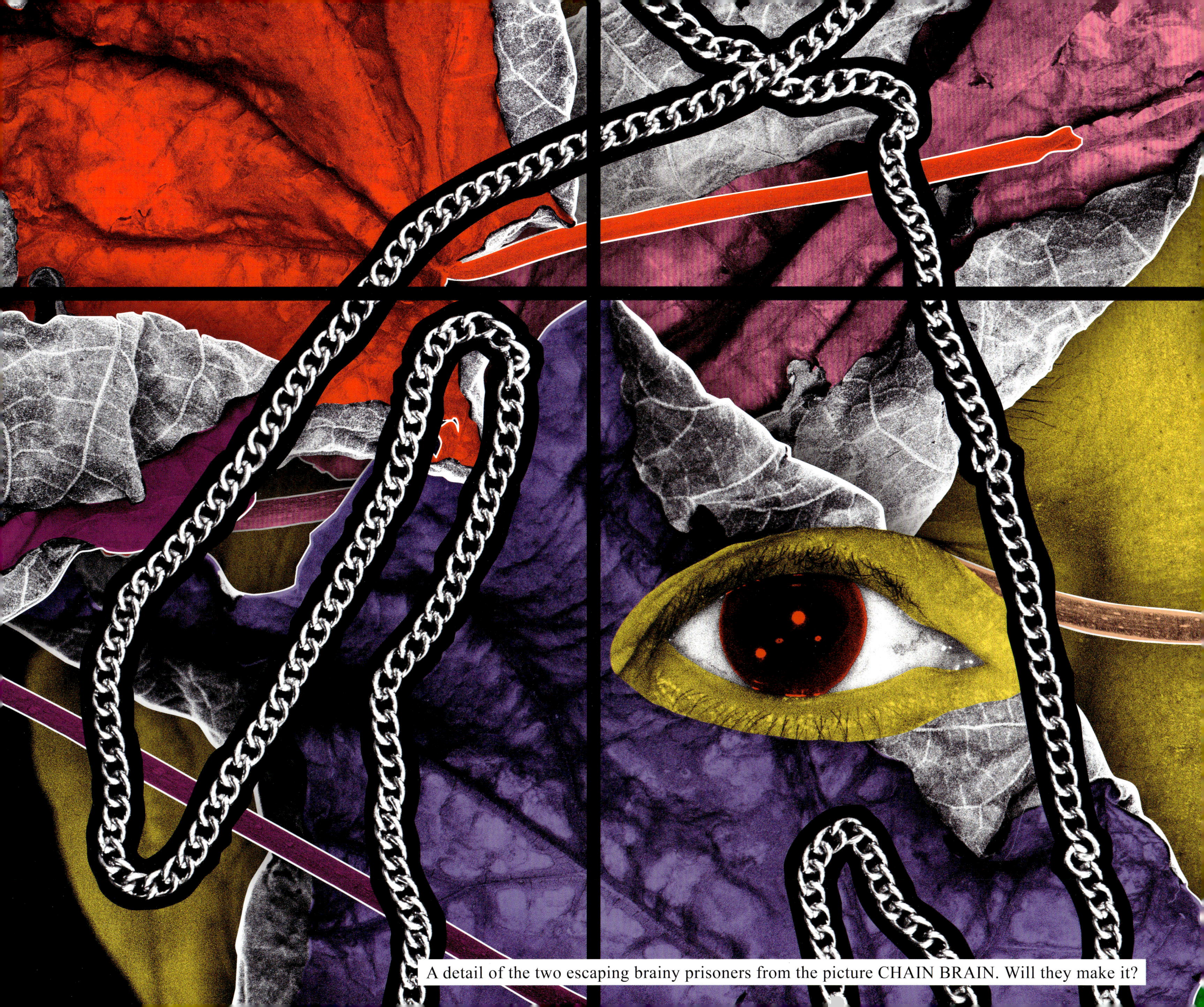

A detail of the two escaping brainy prisoners from the picture CHAIN BRAIN. Will they make it?

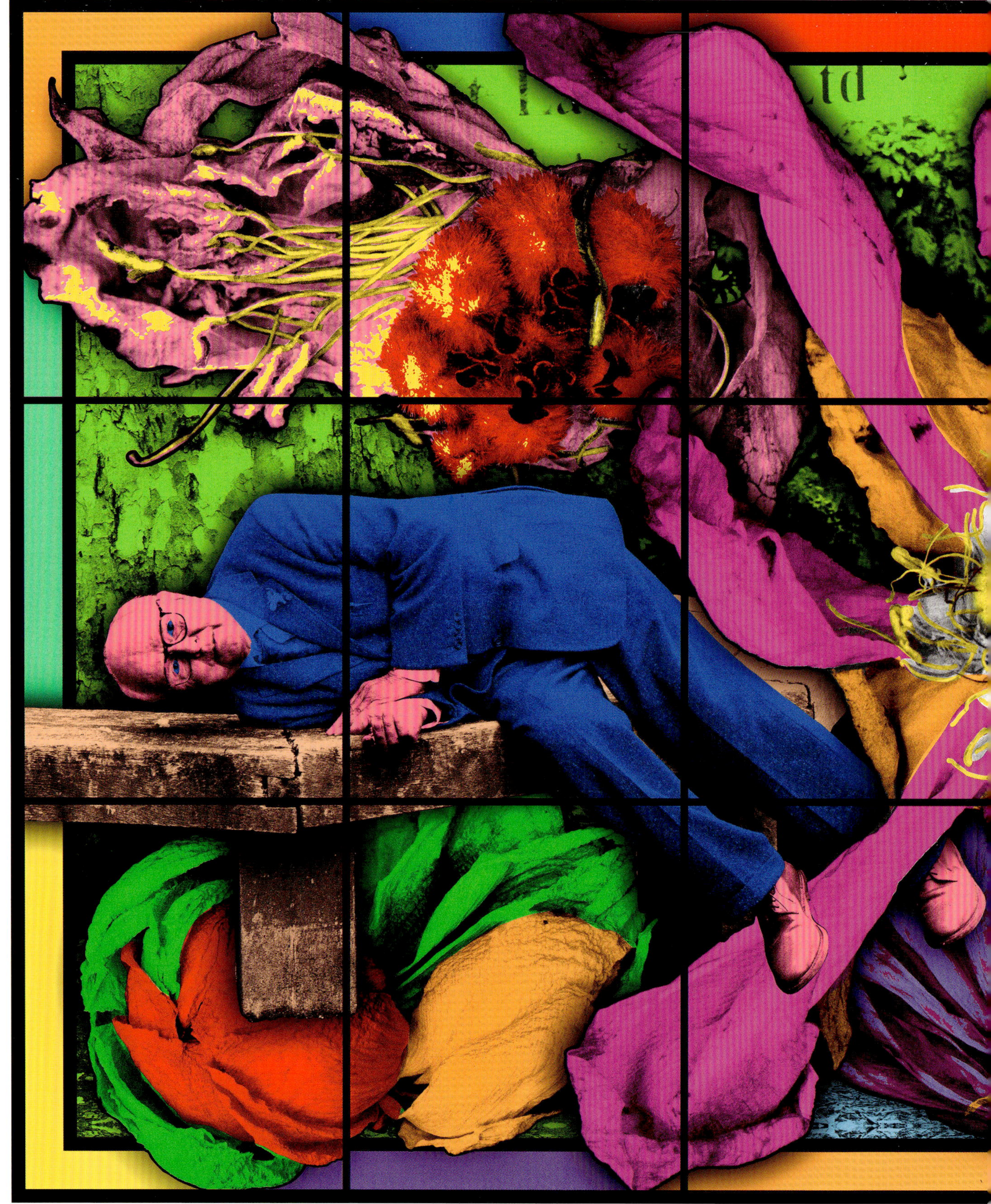

REST. 2019. 89 x 149 inches (226 x 379 cm)

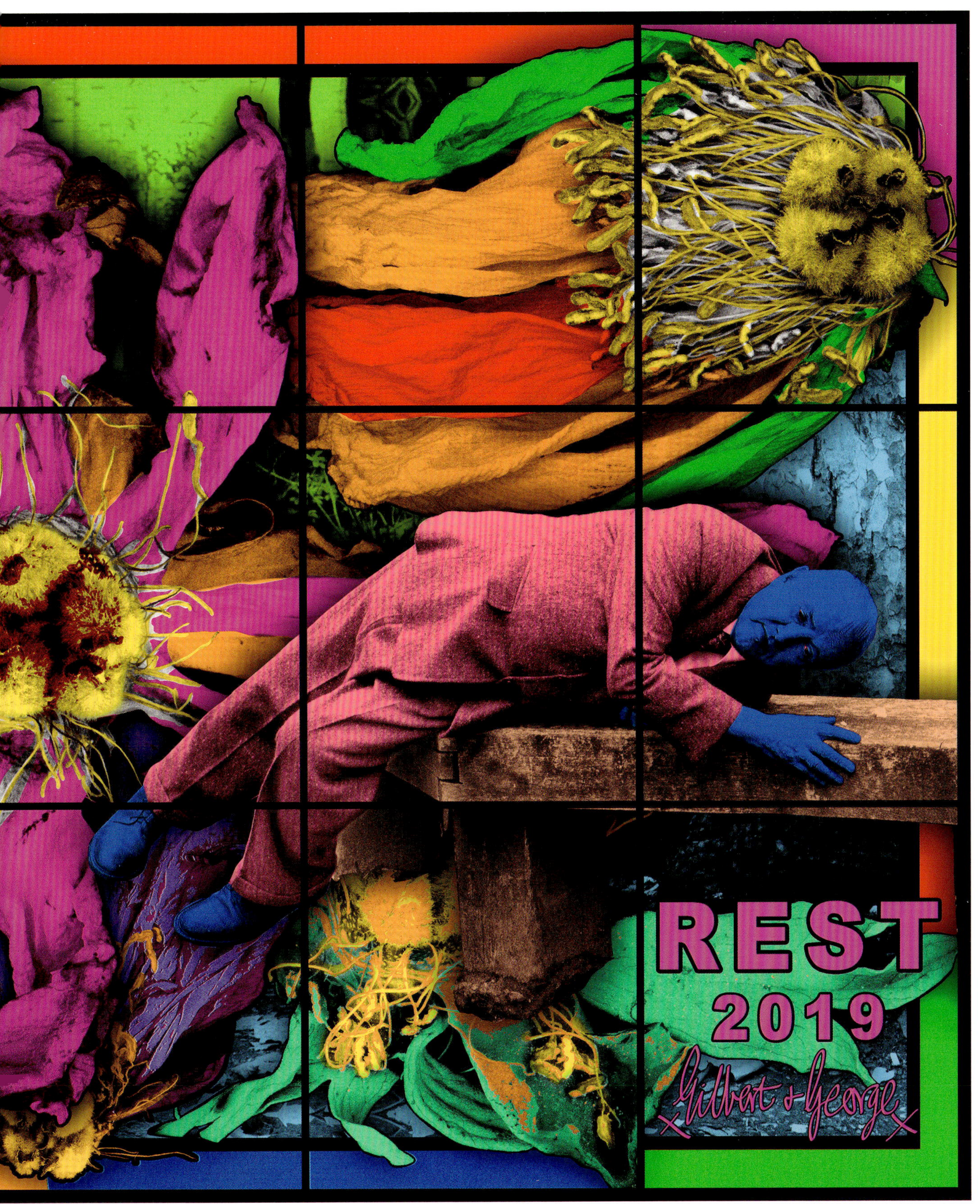
REST
2019
Gilbert & George

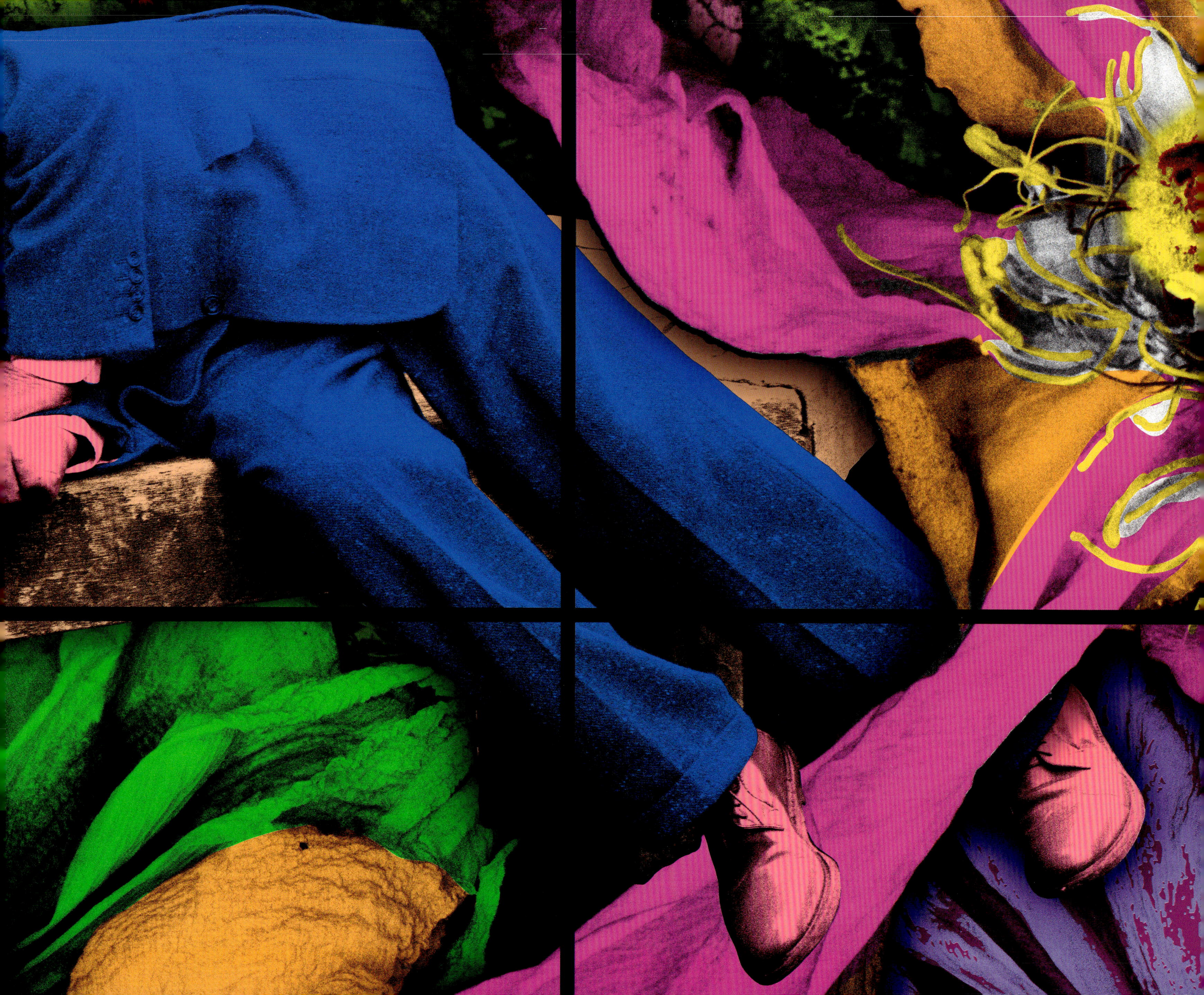

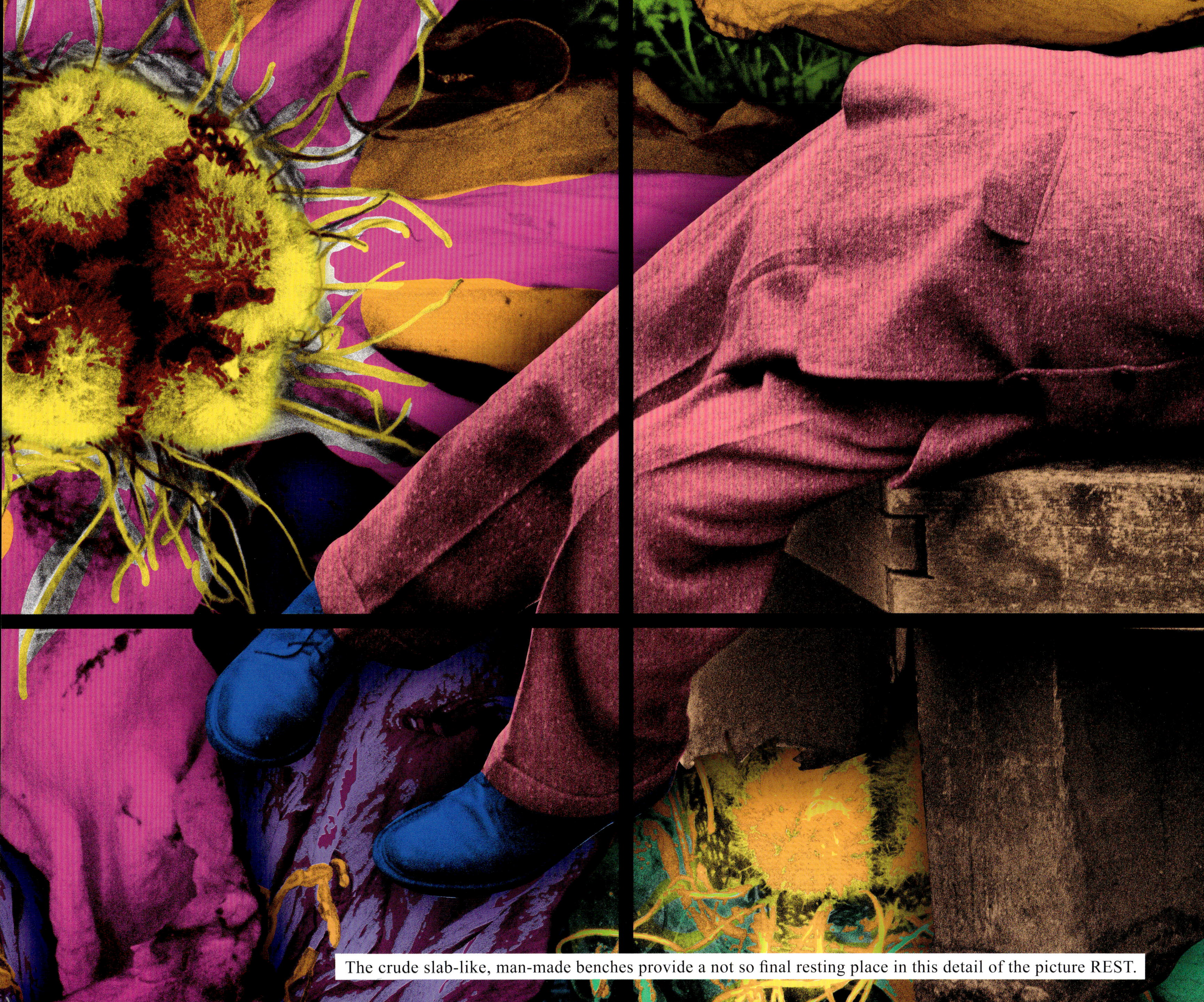

The crude slab-like, man-made benches provide a not so final resting place in this detail of the picture REST.

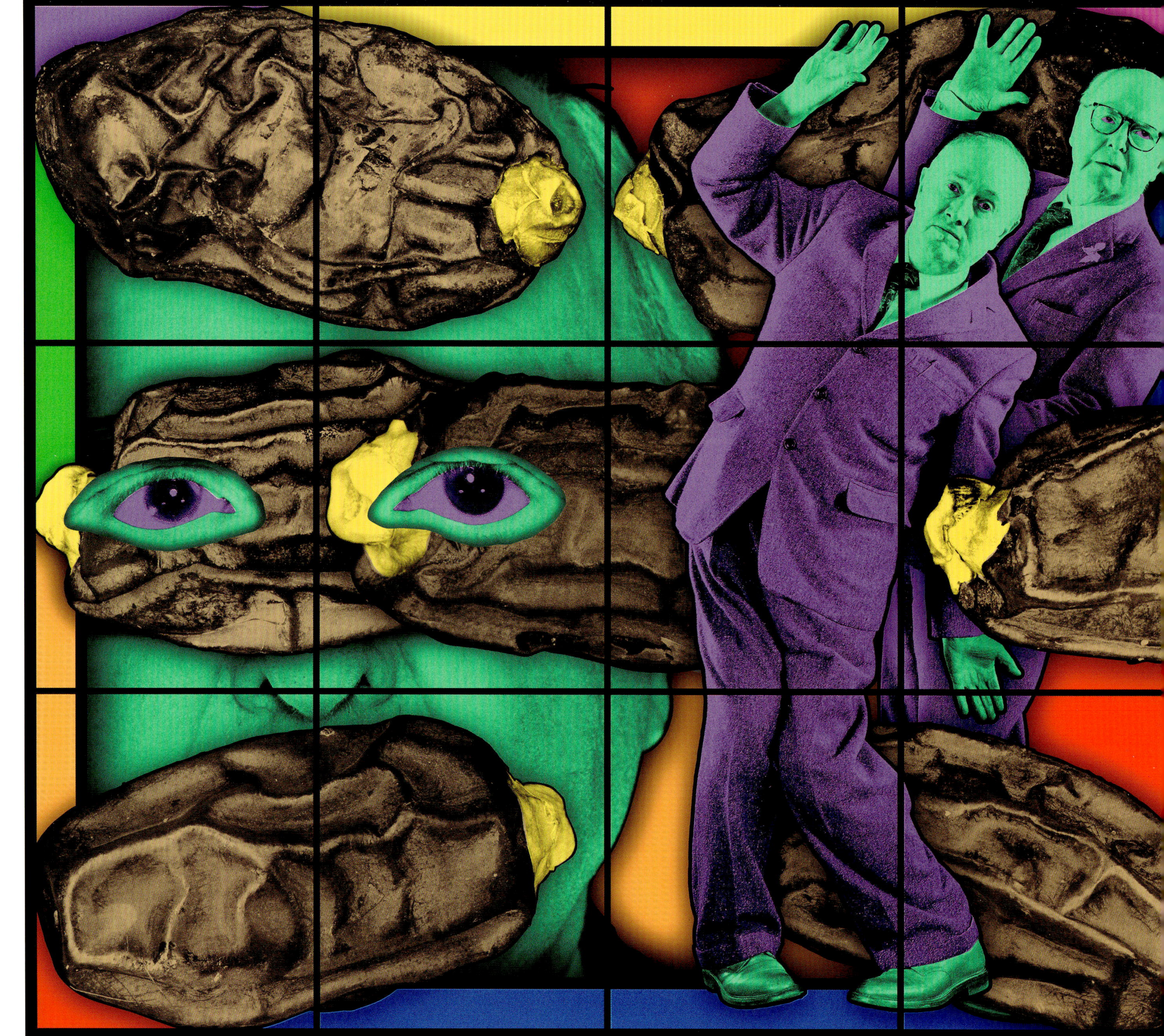

DATE DANCE.
2019.
89 x 199 inches
(226 x 505 cm)

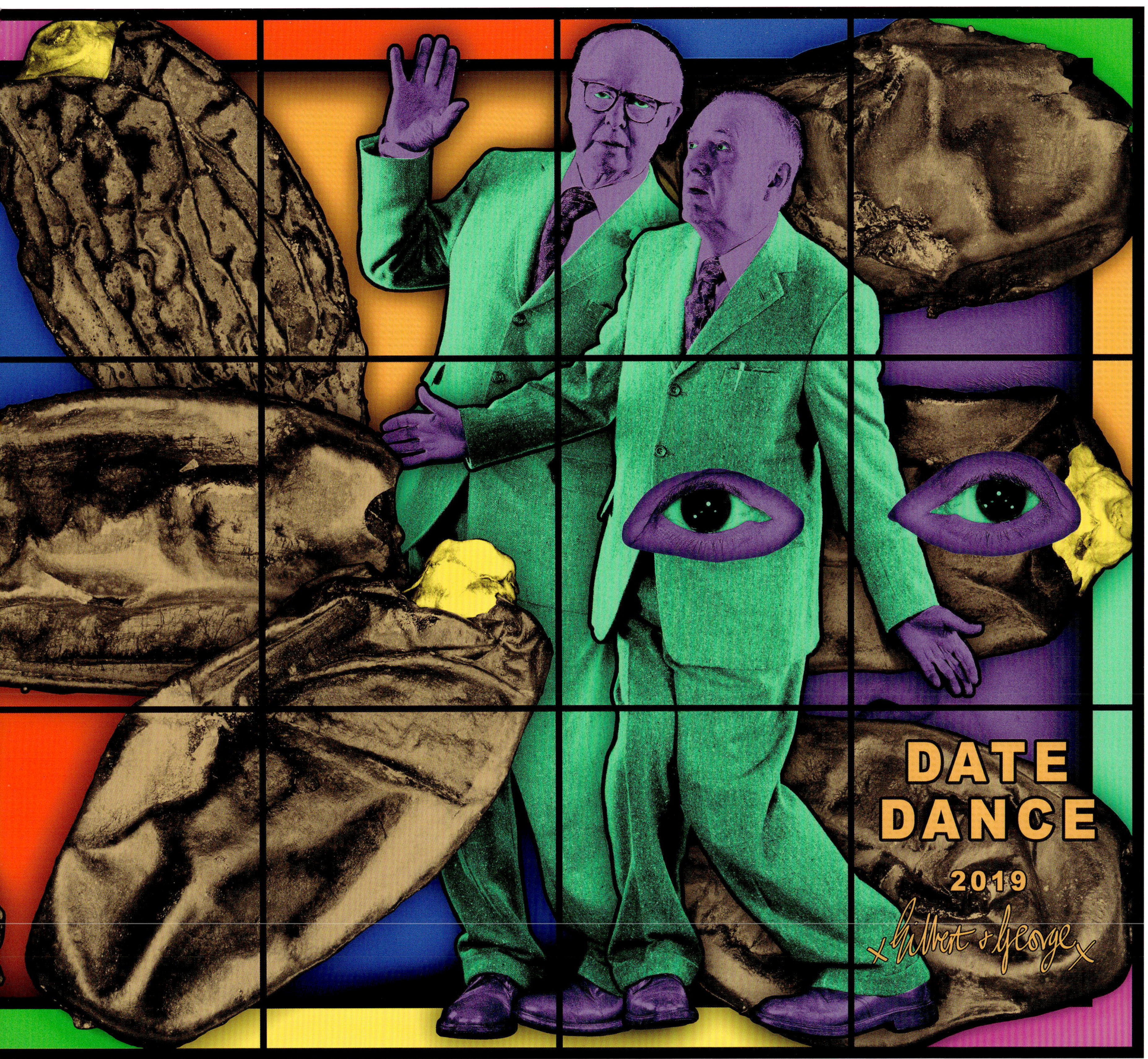
DATE
DANCE
2019
Gilbert & George

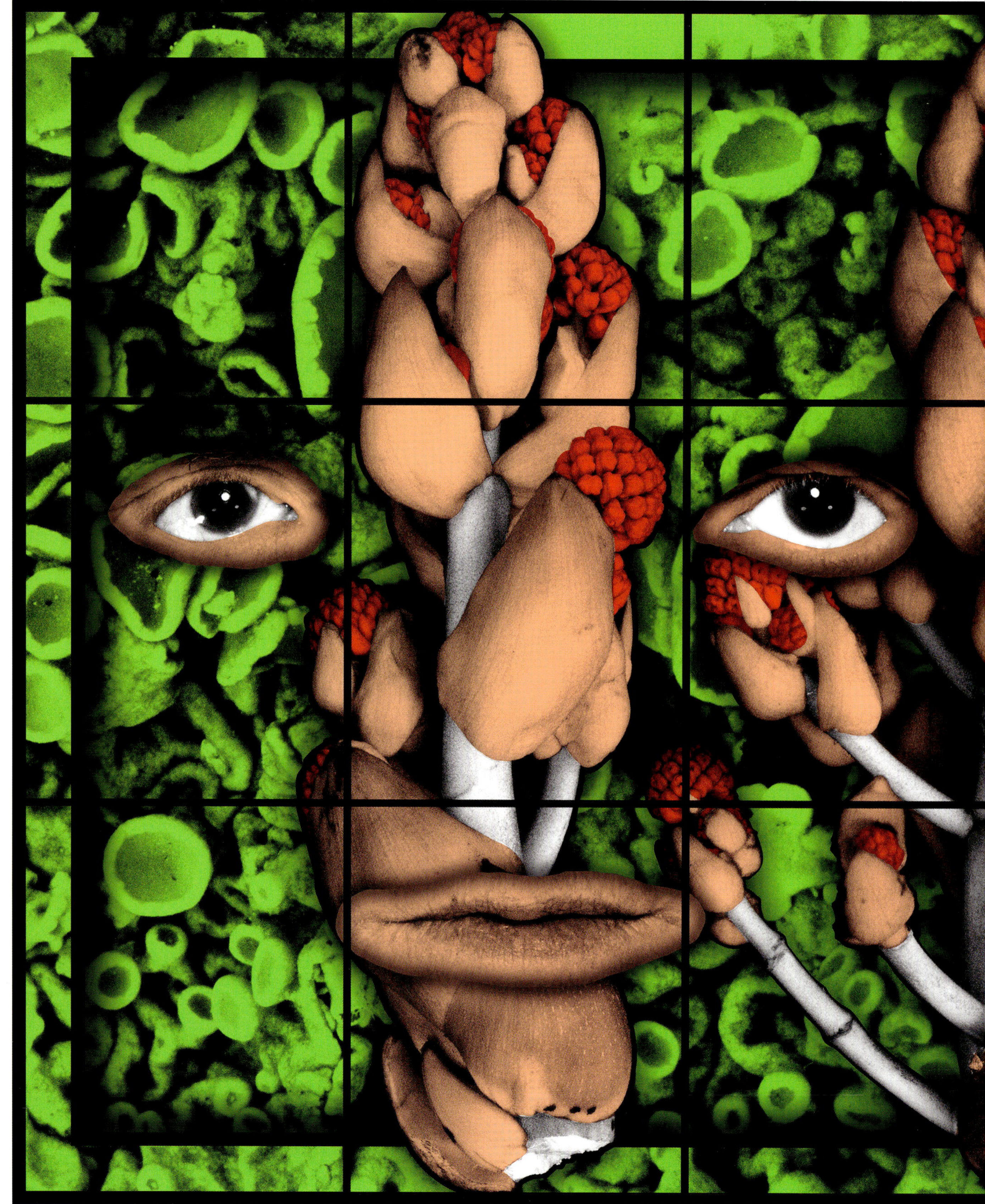

THRICE. 2019. 89 x 149 inches (226 x 379 cm)

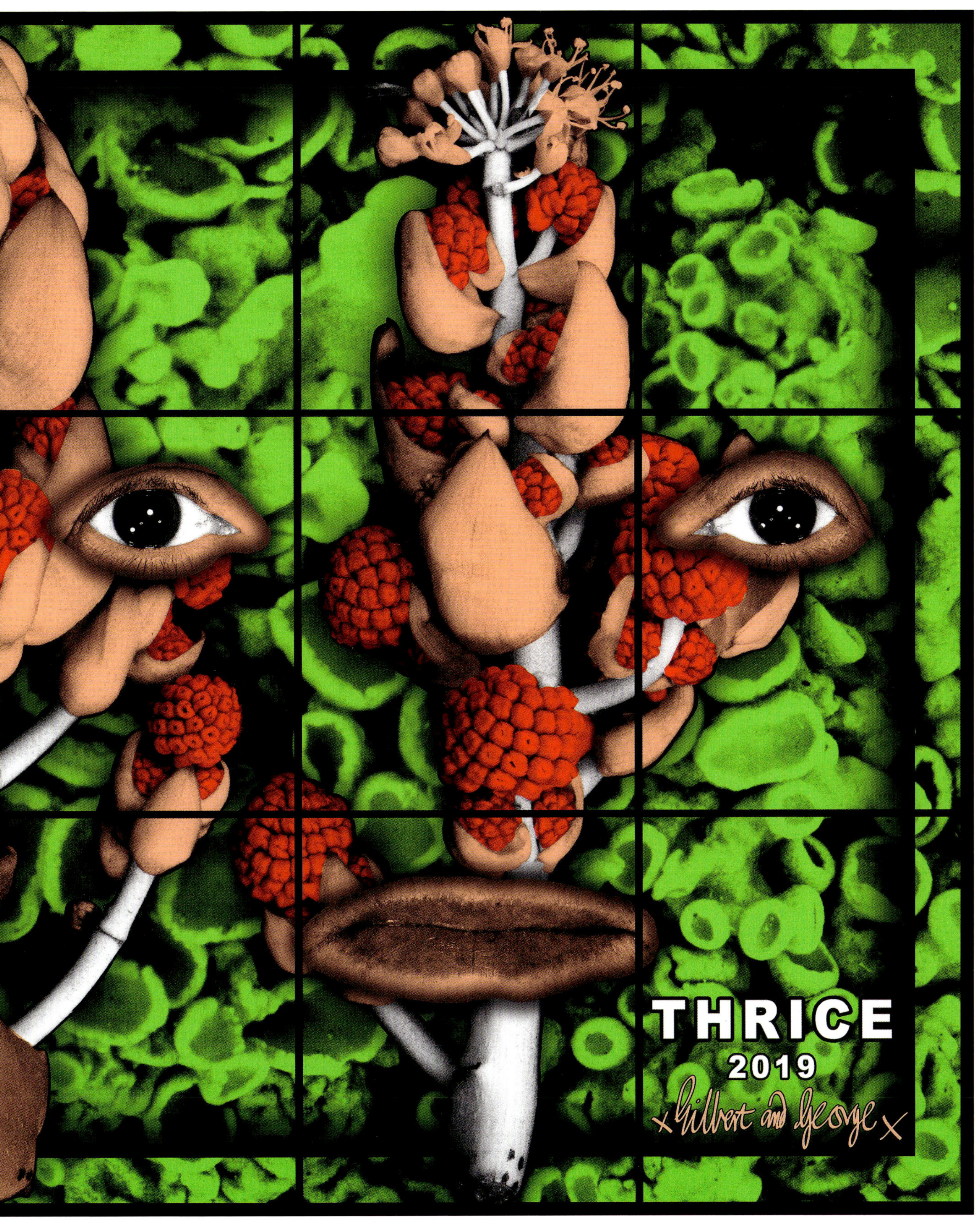
THRICE
2019
Gilbert and George

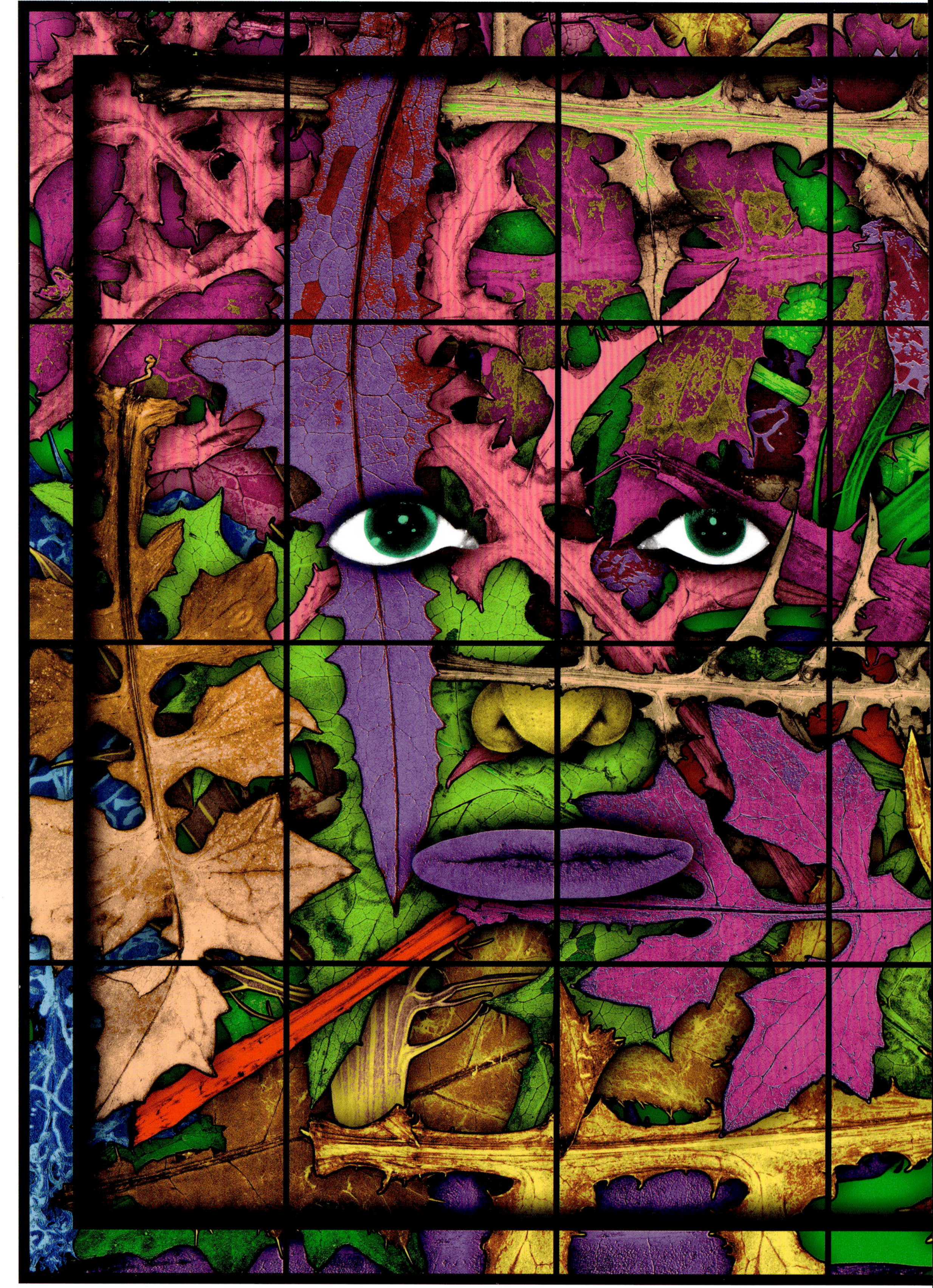

LION TEETH. 2019. 119 x 174 inches (301 x 442 cm)

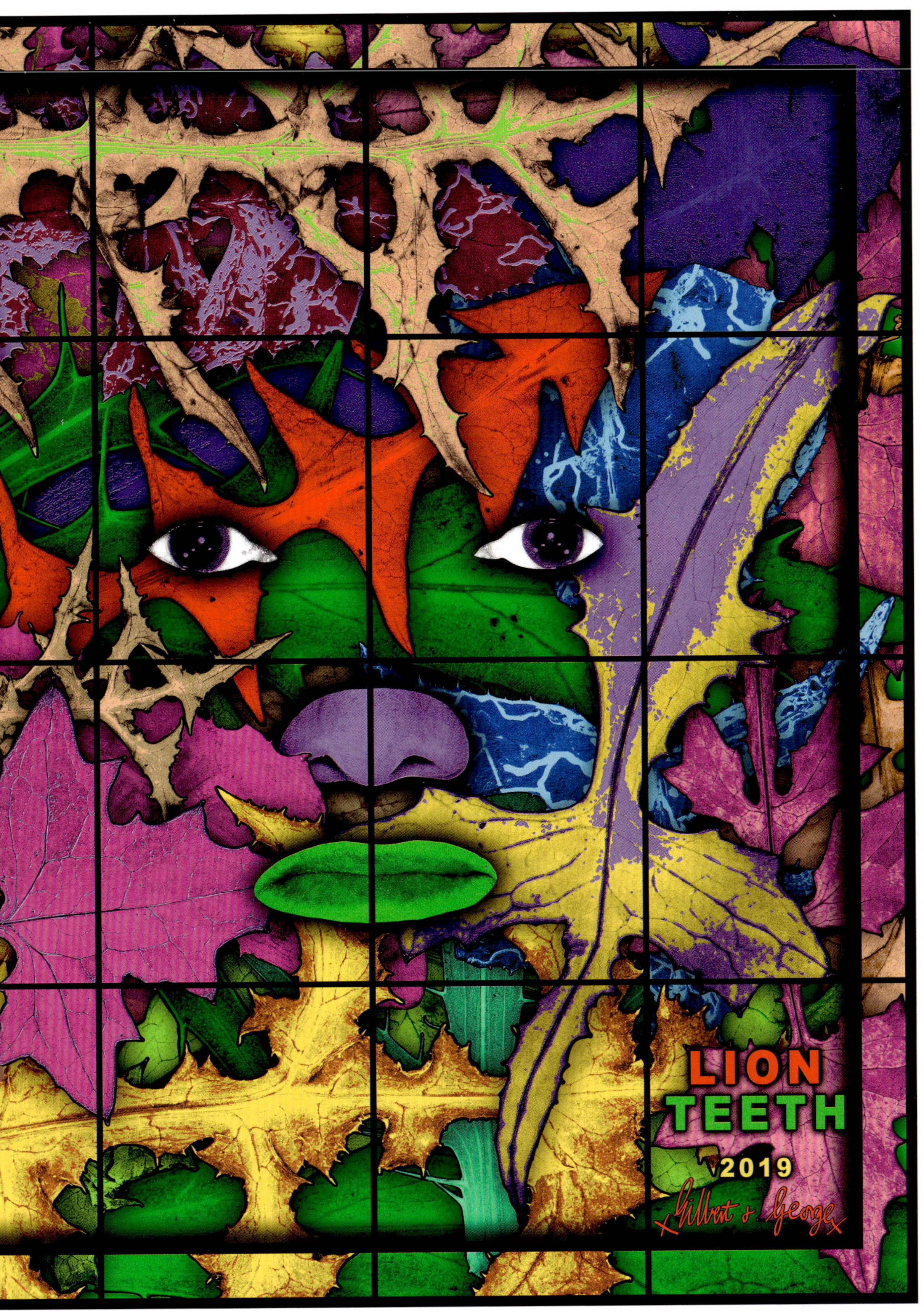
LION
TEETH
2019
Gilbert & George

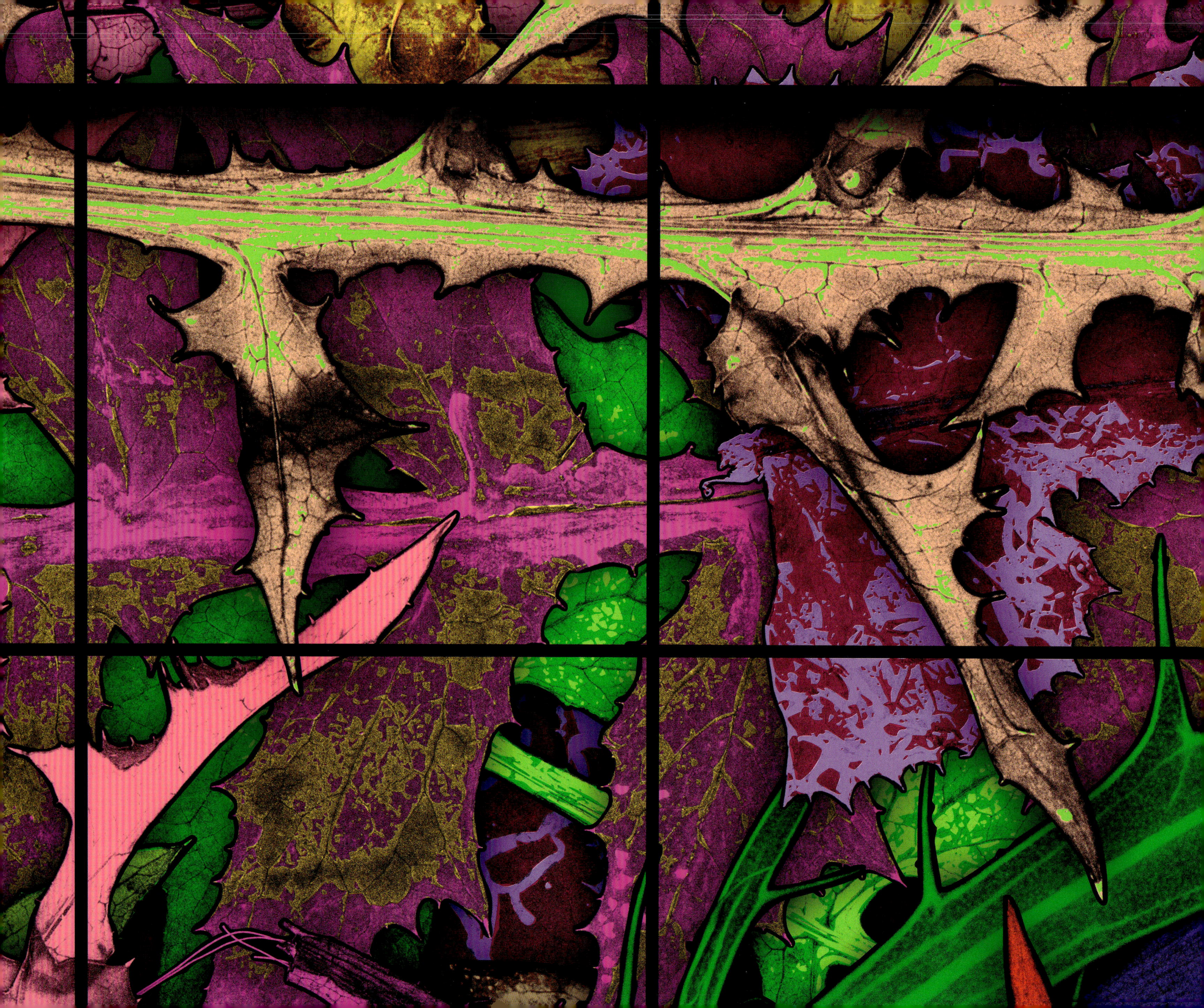

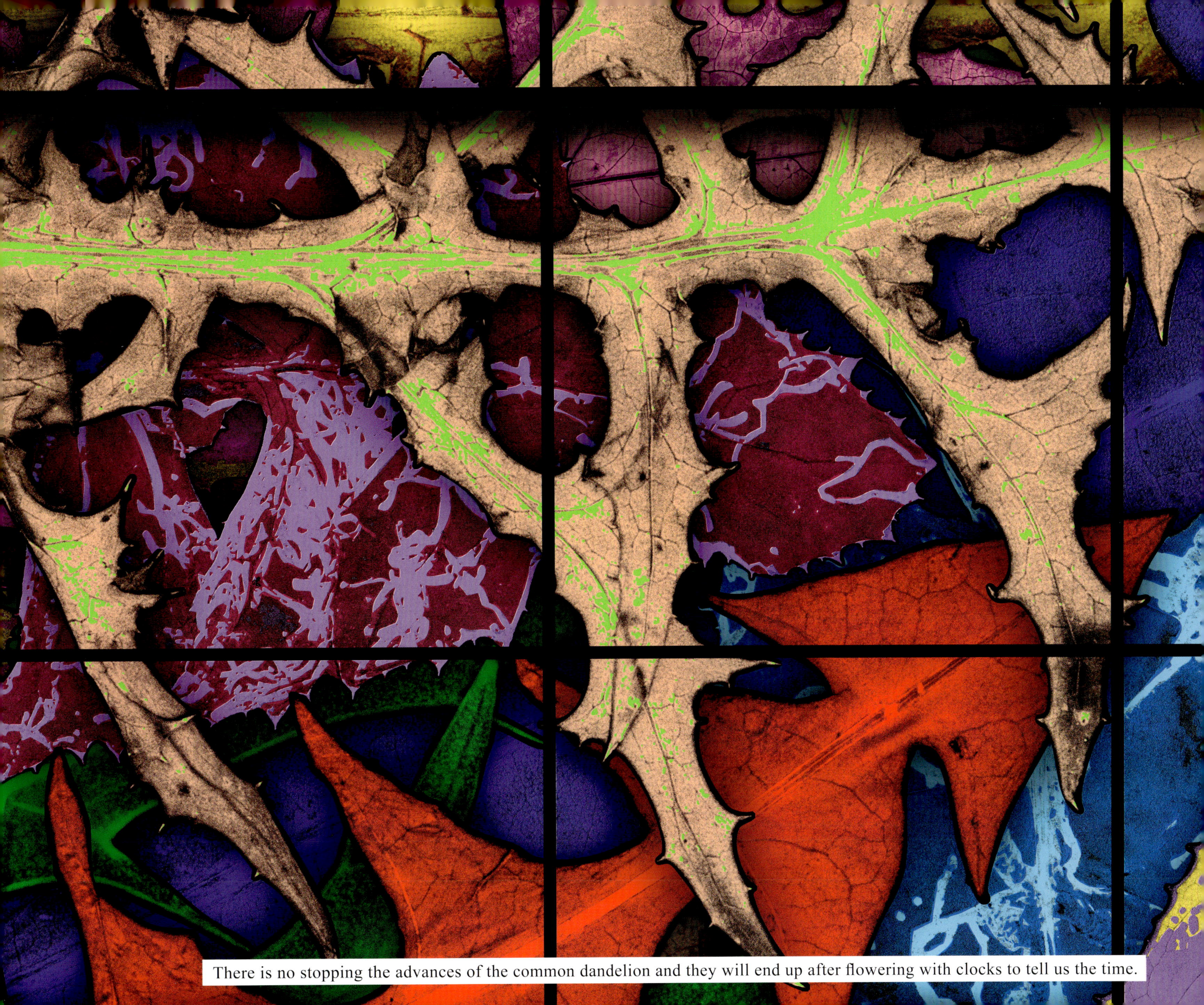

There is no stopping the advances of the common dandelion and they will end up after flowering with clocks to tell us the time.

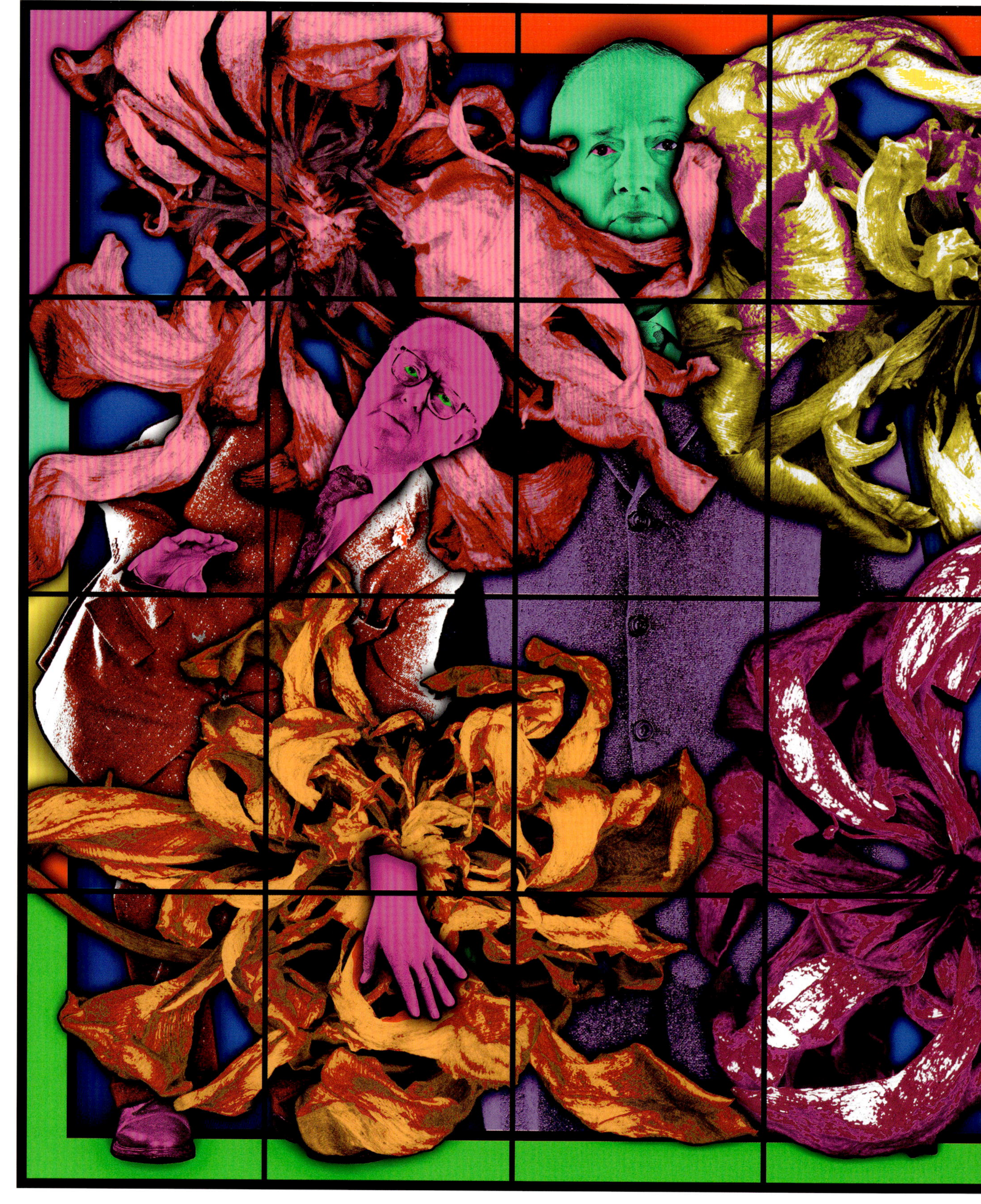

SEXPARTITE. 2019.
119 x 199 inches (301 x 505 cm)

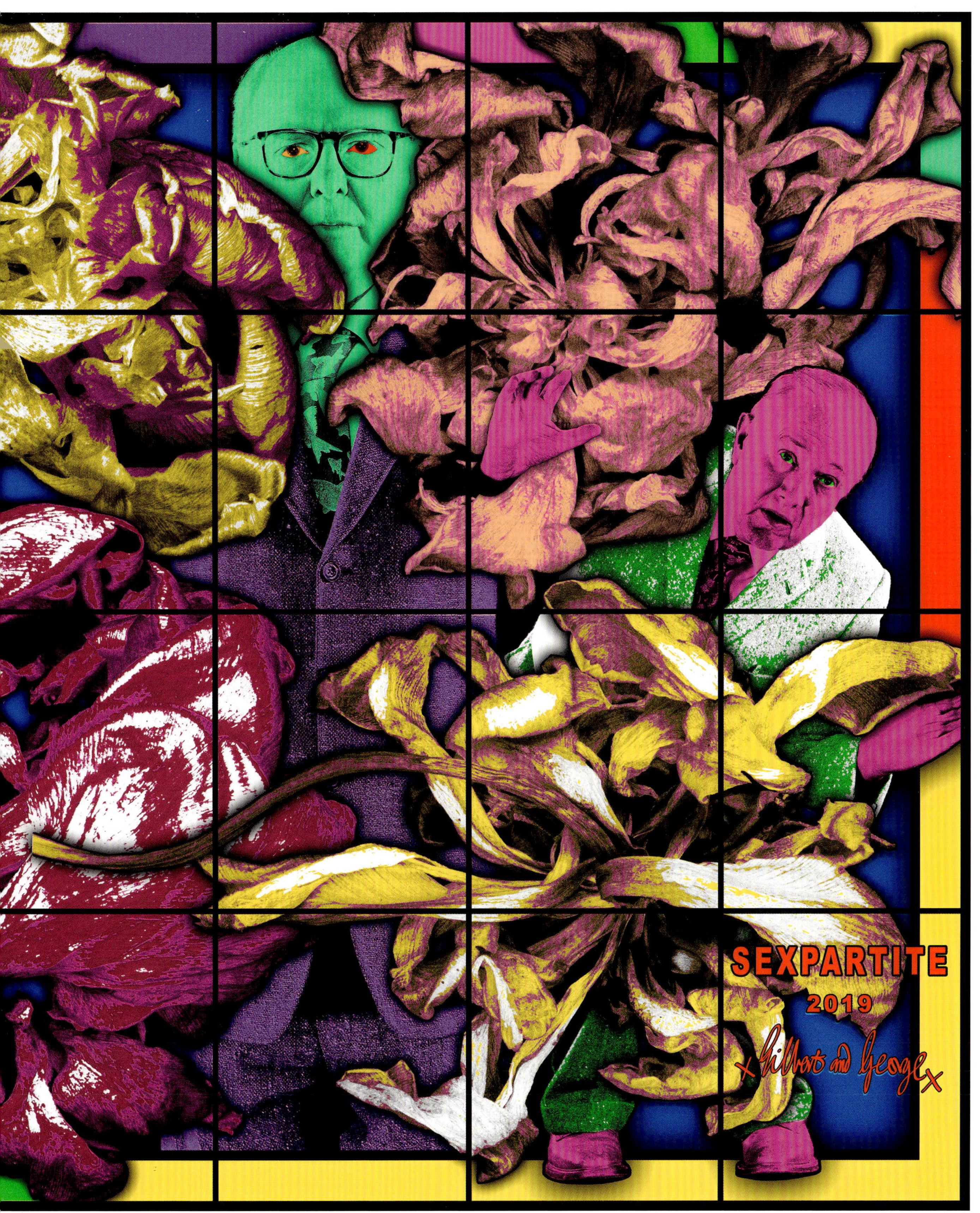
SEXPARTITE
2019
Gilbert and George

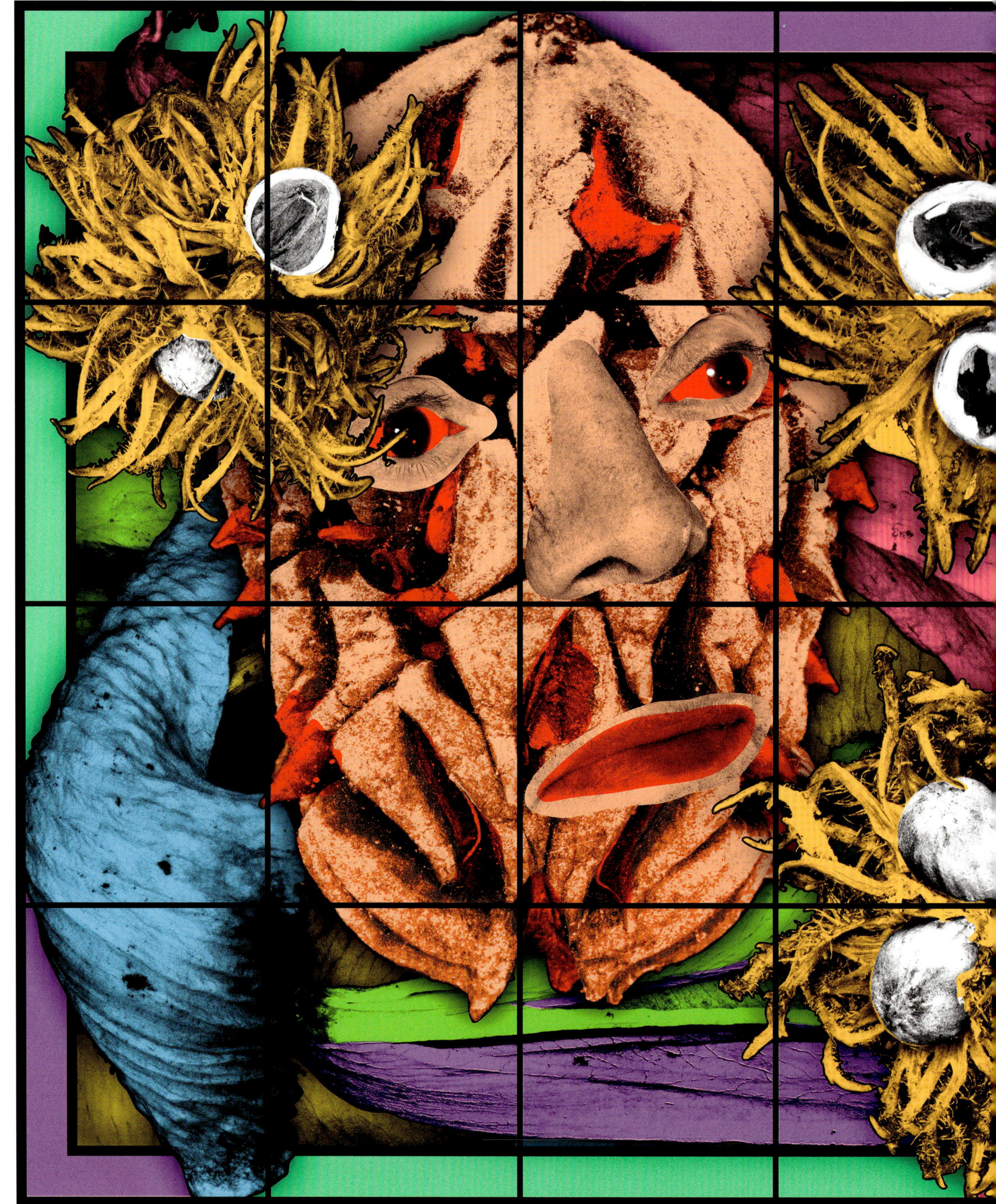

MAGNOLIA HEADS. 2019.
119 x 199 inches (301 x 505 cm)

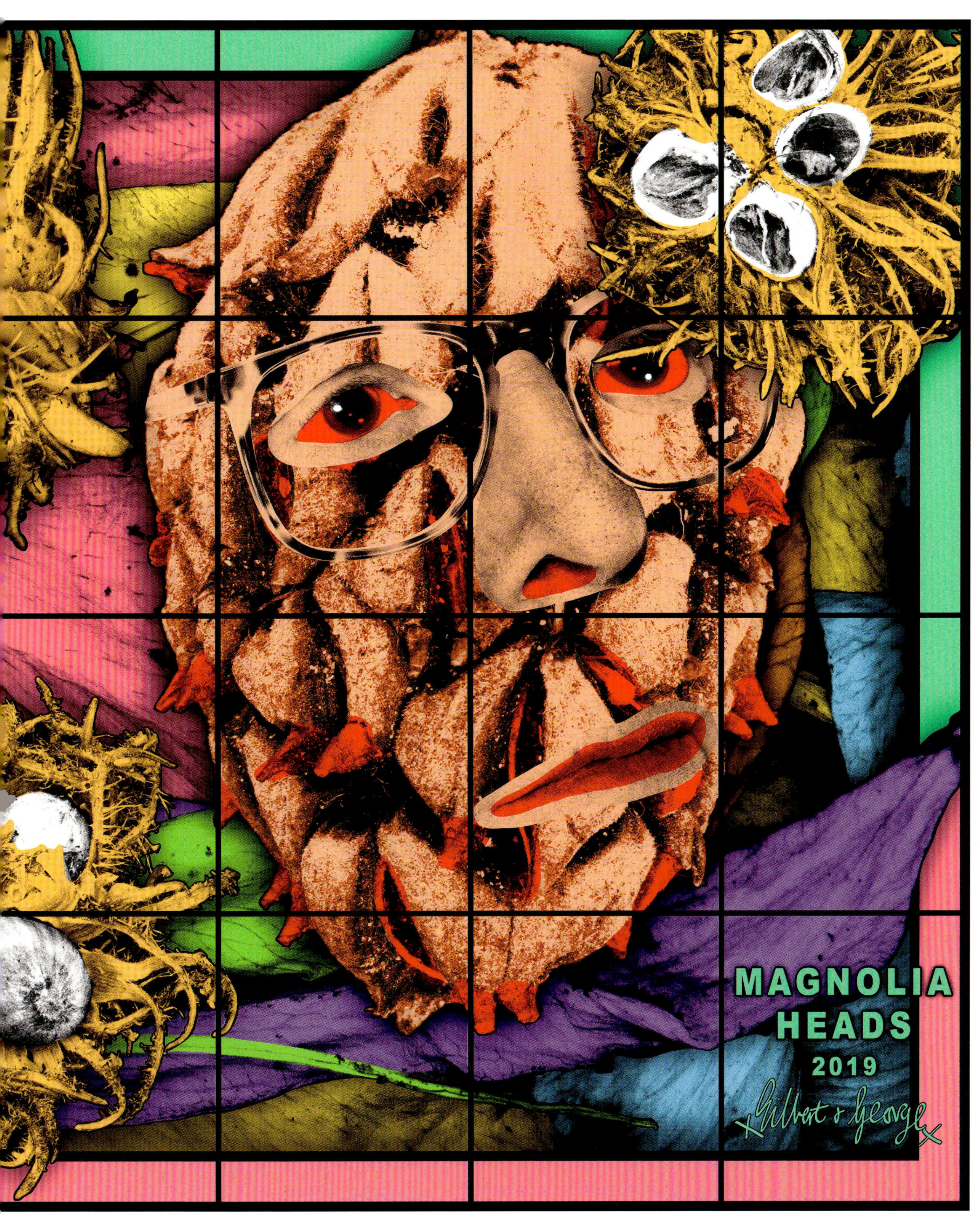
MAGNOLIA
HEADS
2019
Gilbert & George

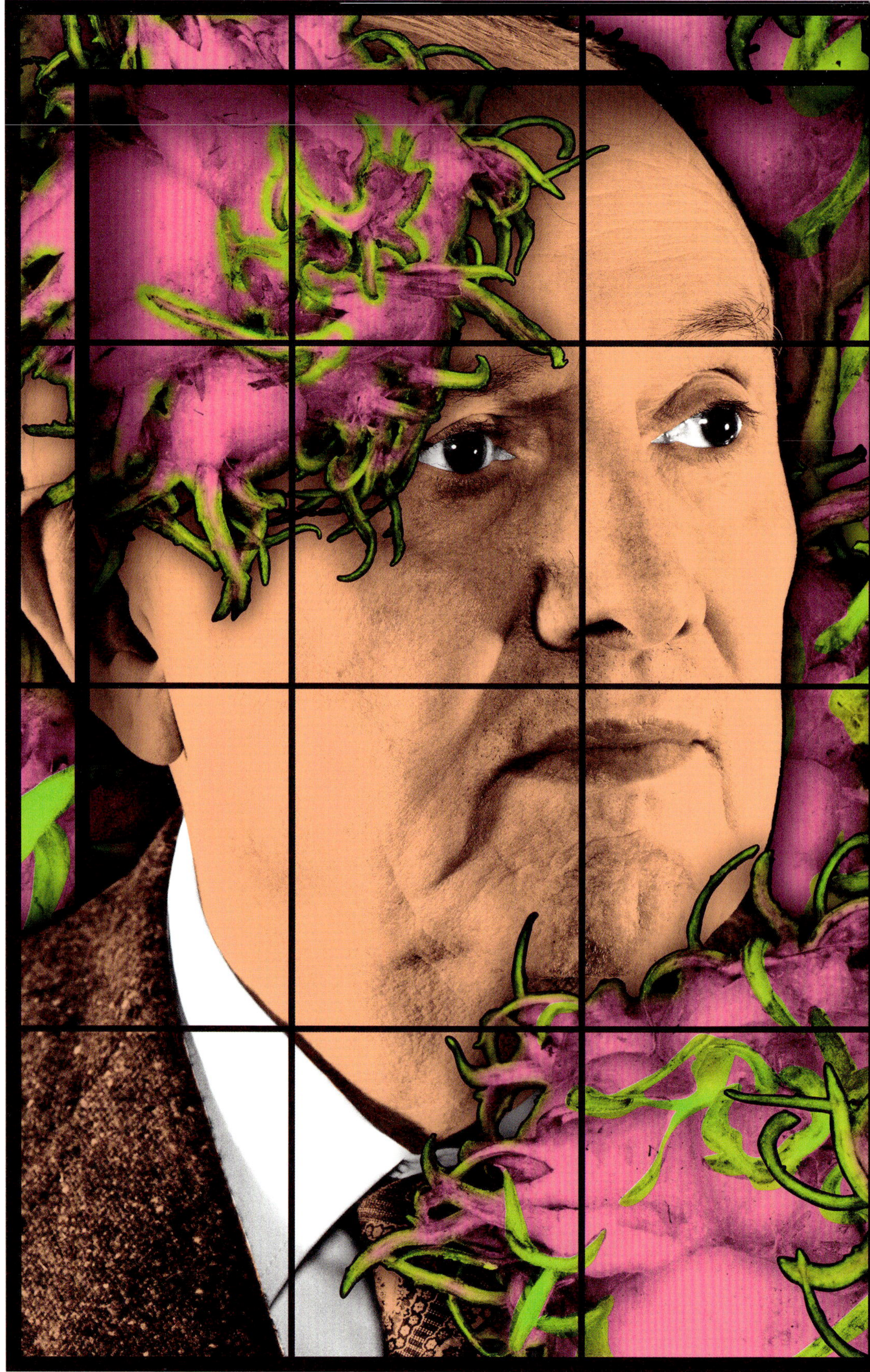

ON THE BENCH. 2019. 119 x 224 inches (301 x 568 cm)

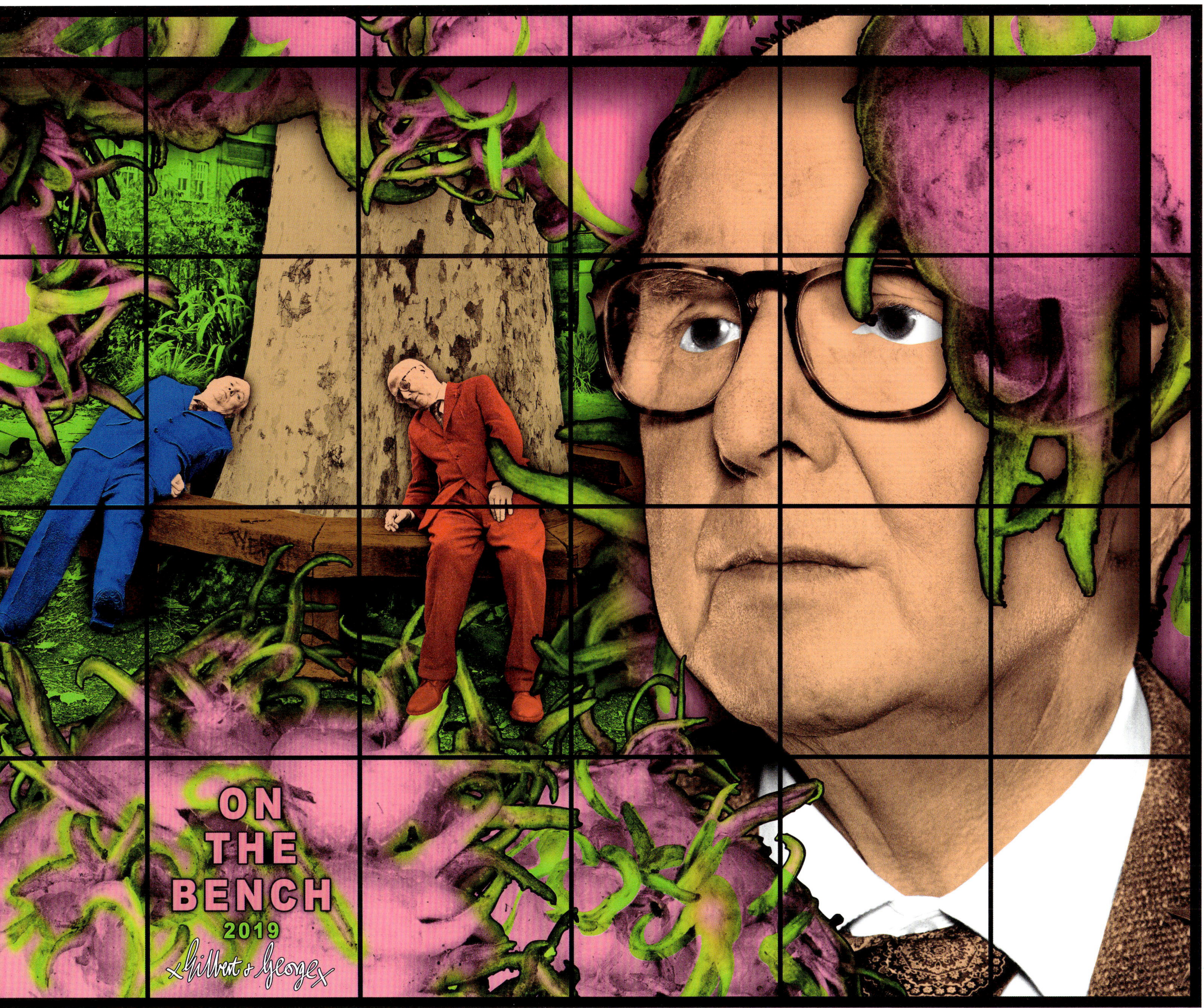
ON
THE
BENCH
2019
Gilbert & George

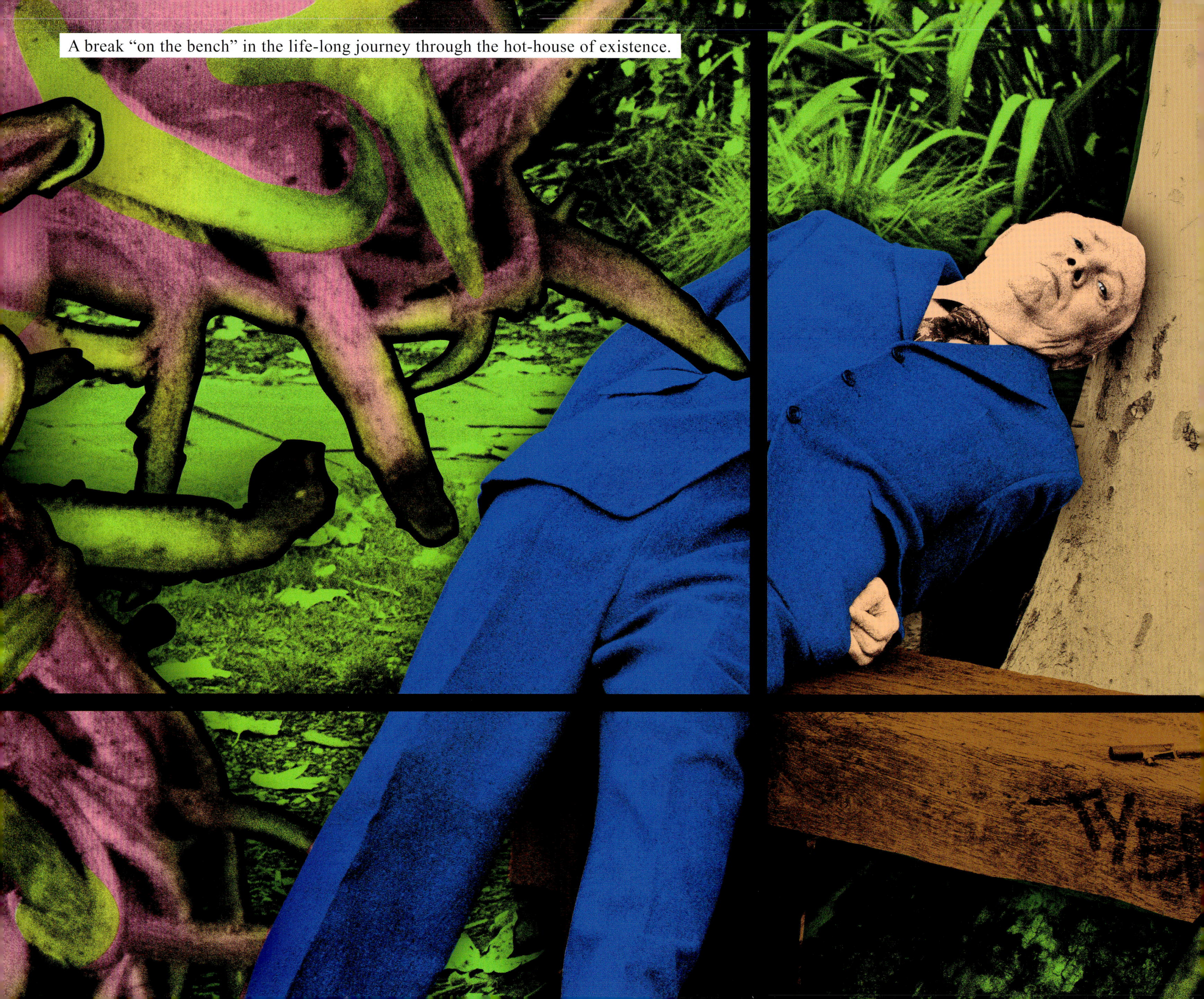

A break “on the bench” in the life-long journey through the hot-house of existence.

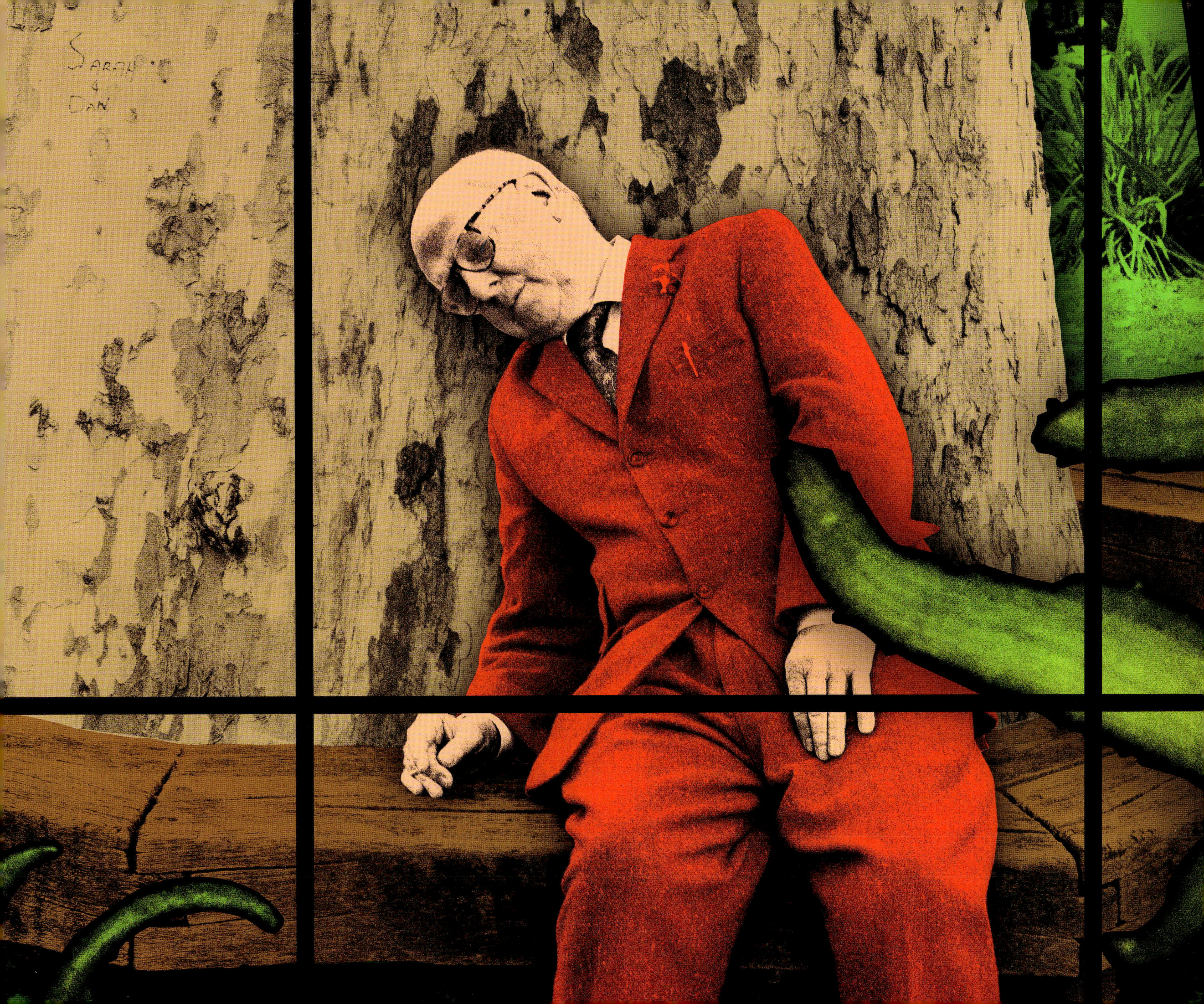
SARAH
4
DAN

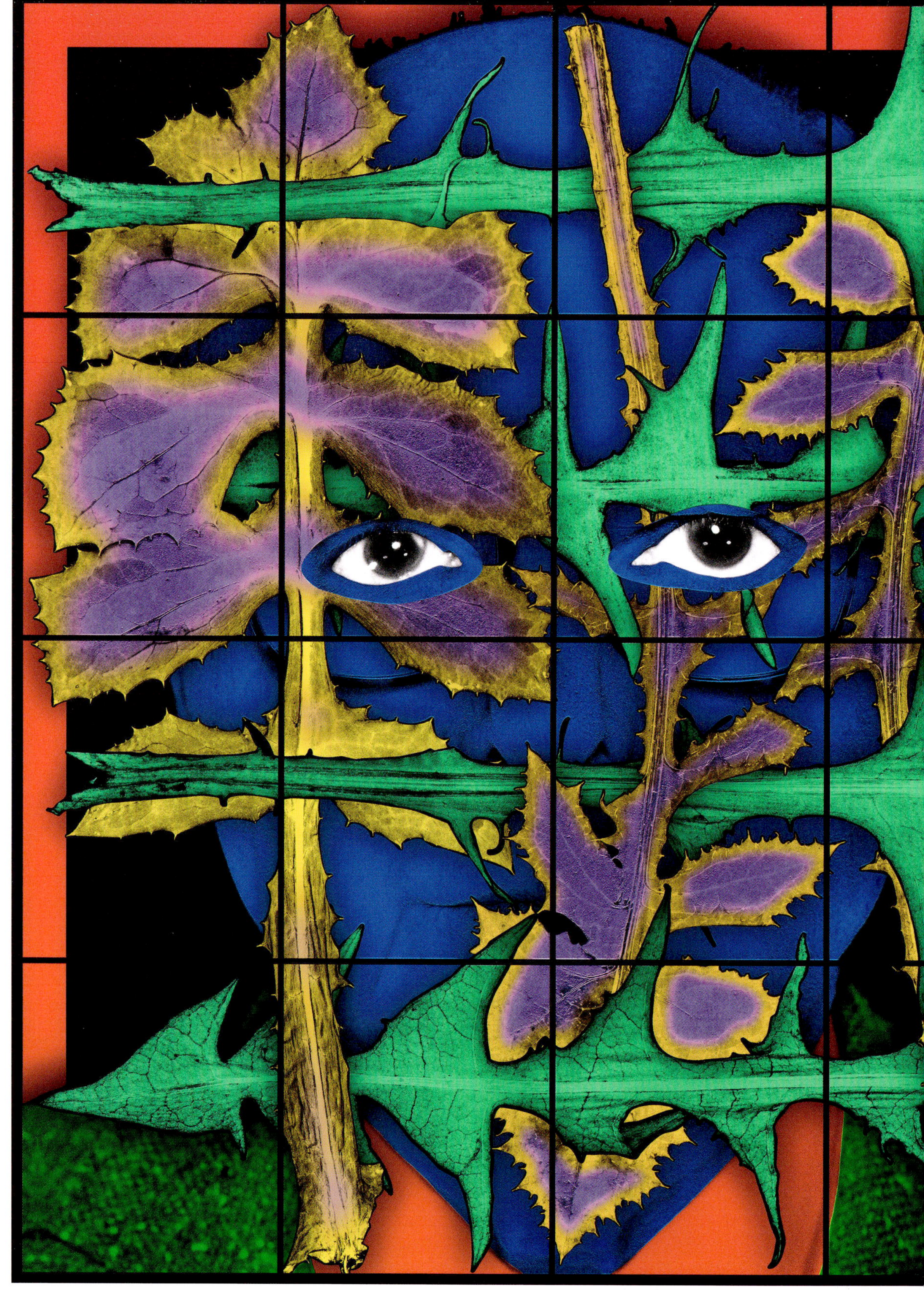

DENT-DE-LION. 2019. 119 x 174 inches (301 x 442 cm)

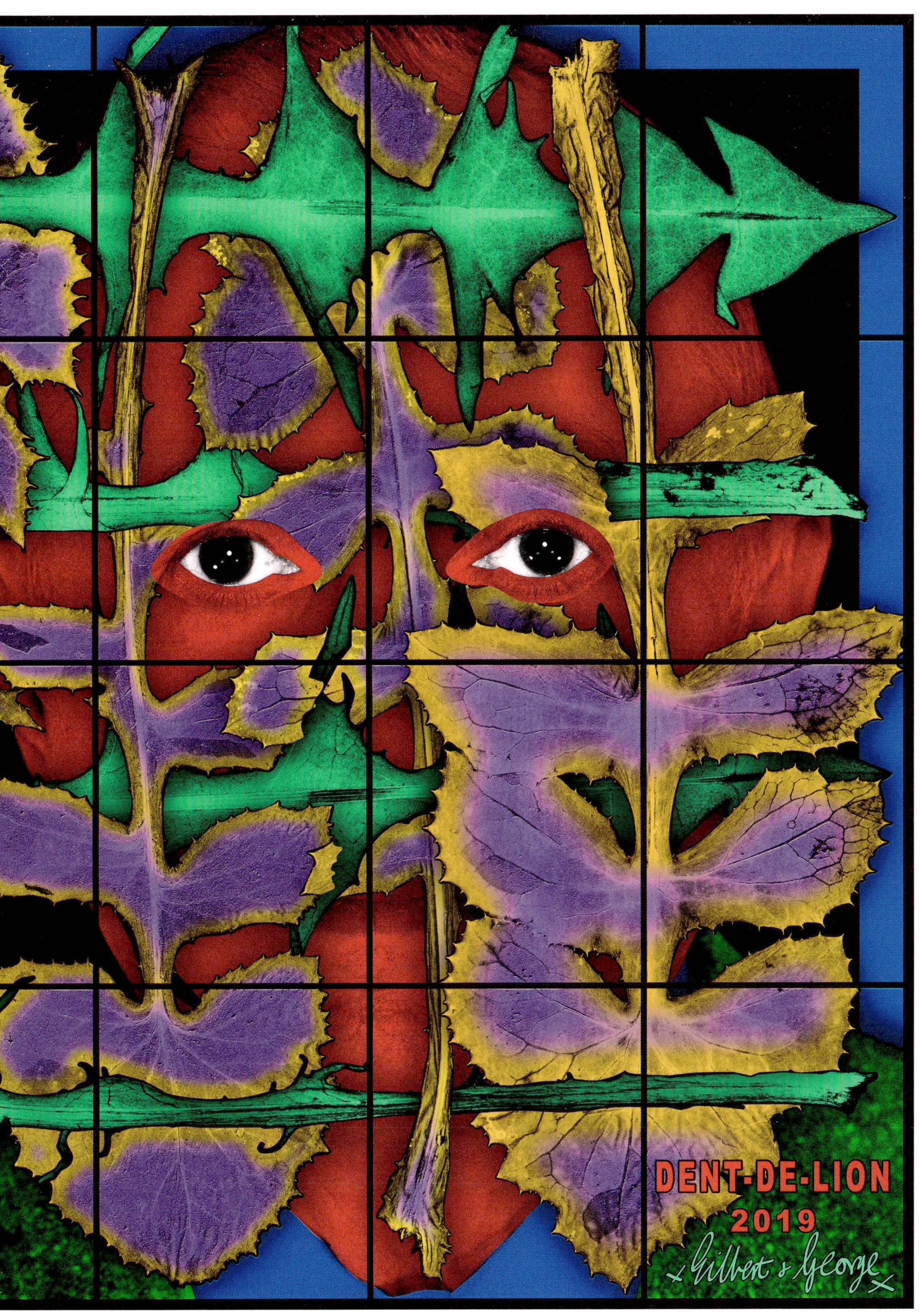
DENT-DE-LION
2019
Gilbert & George

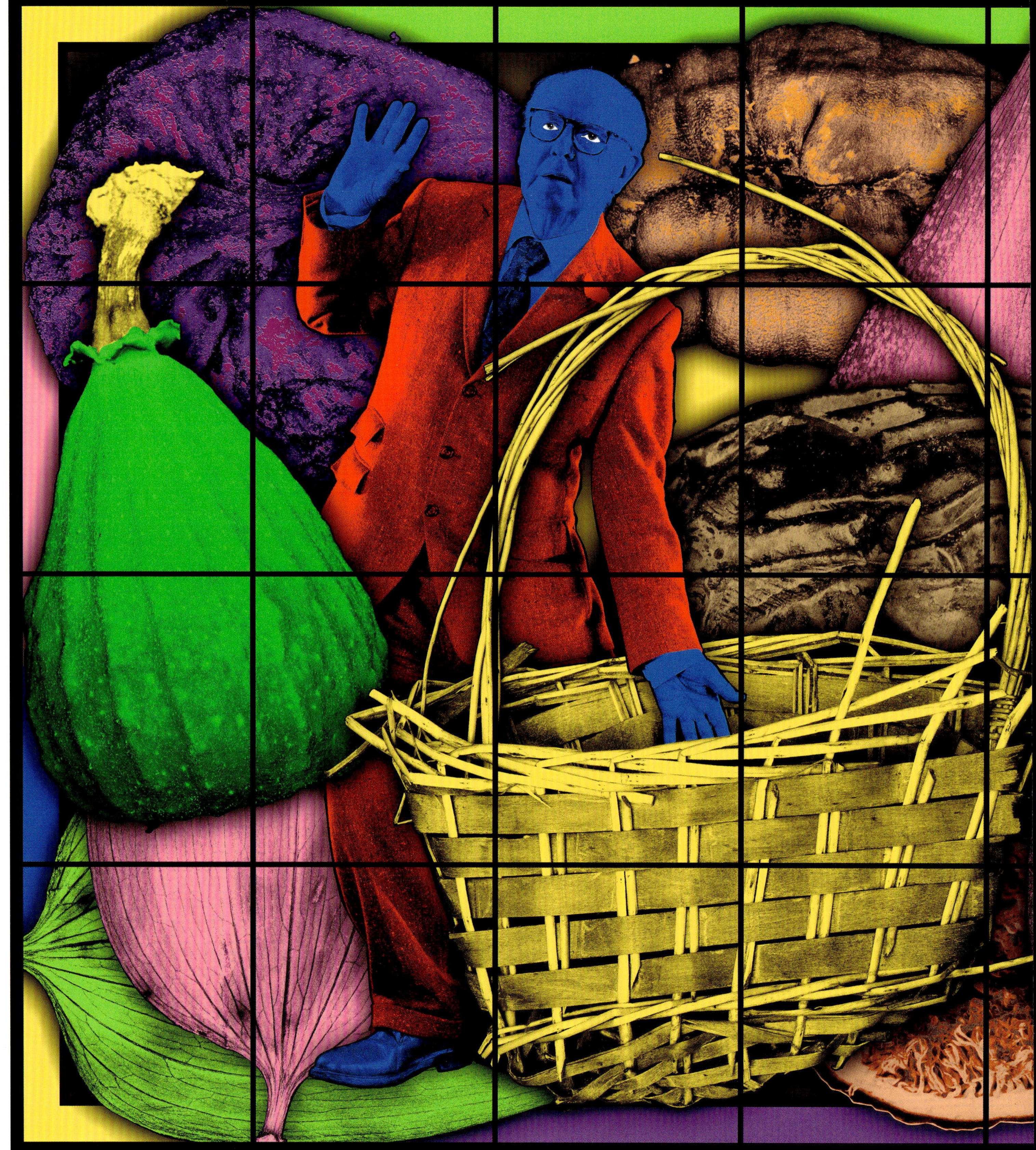

GOLD BASKET. 2019.
119 x 224 inches (301 x 568 cm)

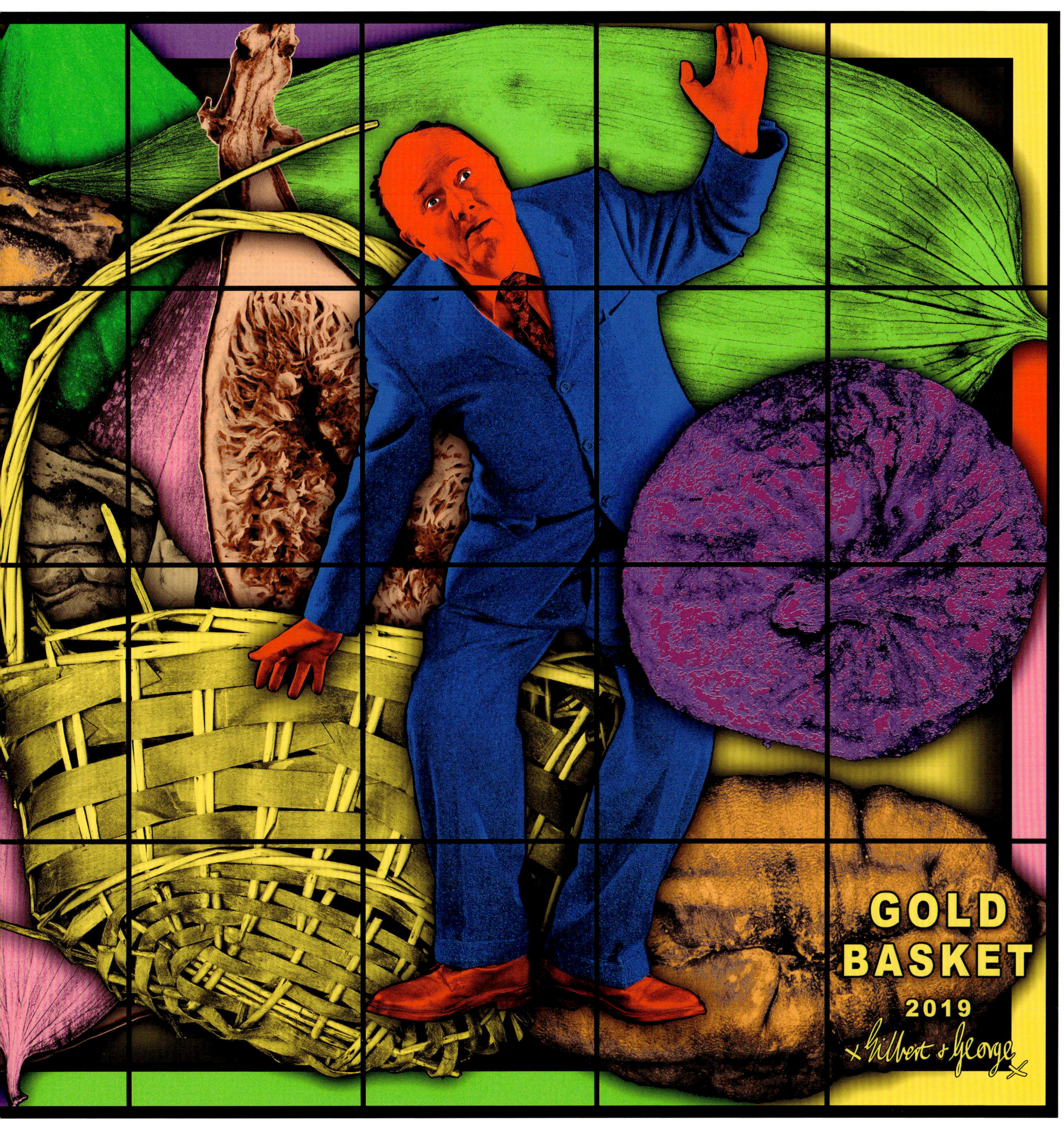
GOLD
BASKET
2019
Gilbert & George

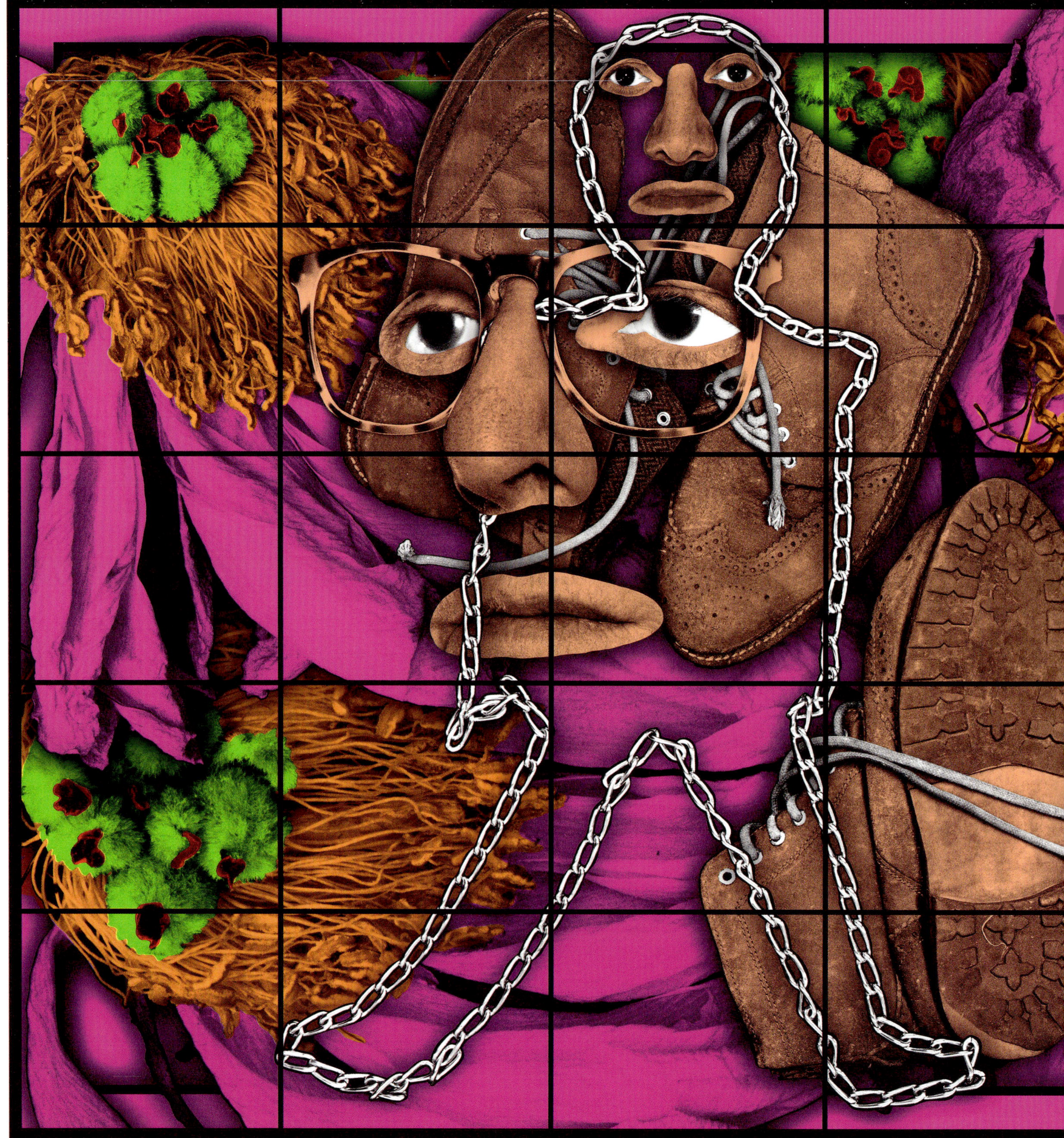

BOOTS. 2019.
125 x 266 inches (316 x 676 cm)

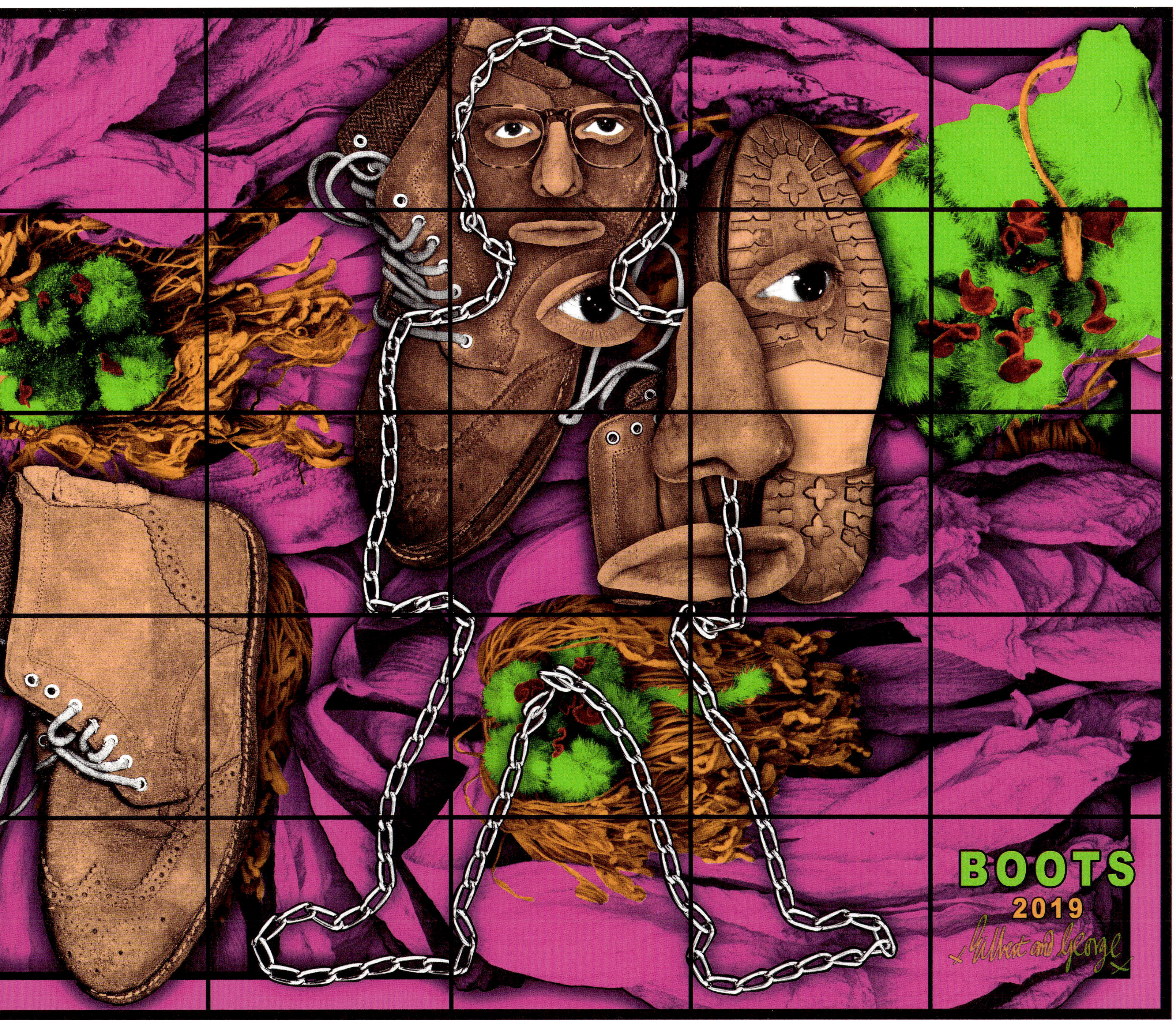
BOOTS
2019
Gilbert and George

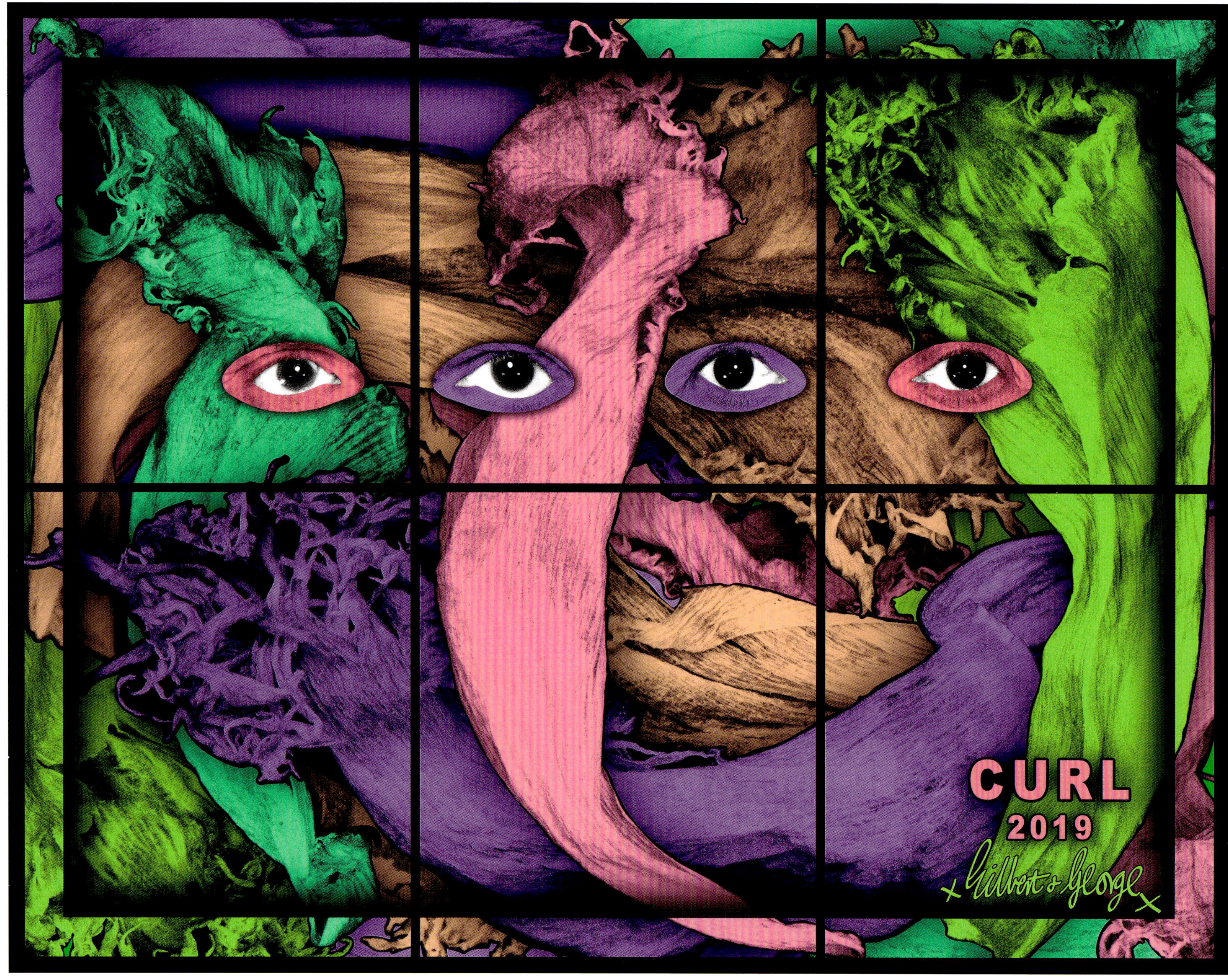

CURL. 2019. 60 x 75 inches (151 x 190 cm)

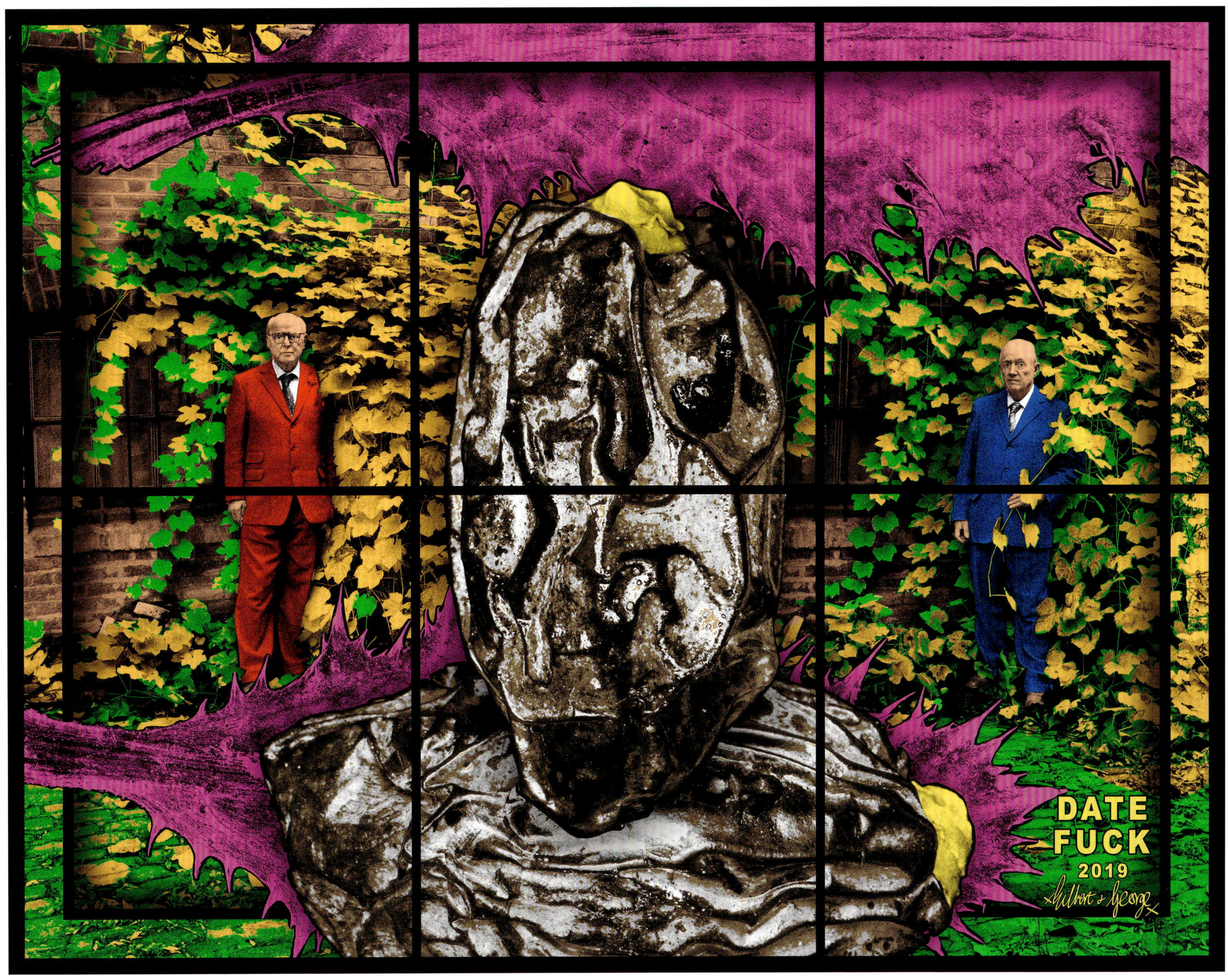

DATE FUCK. 2019. 60 x 75 inches (151 x 190 cm)

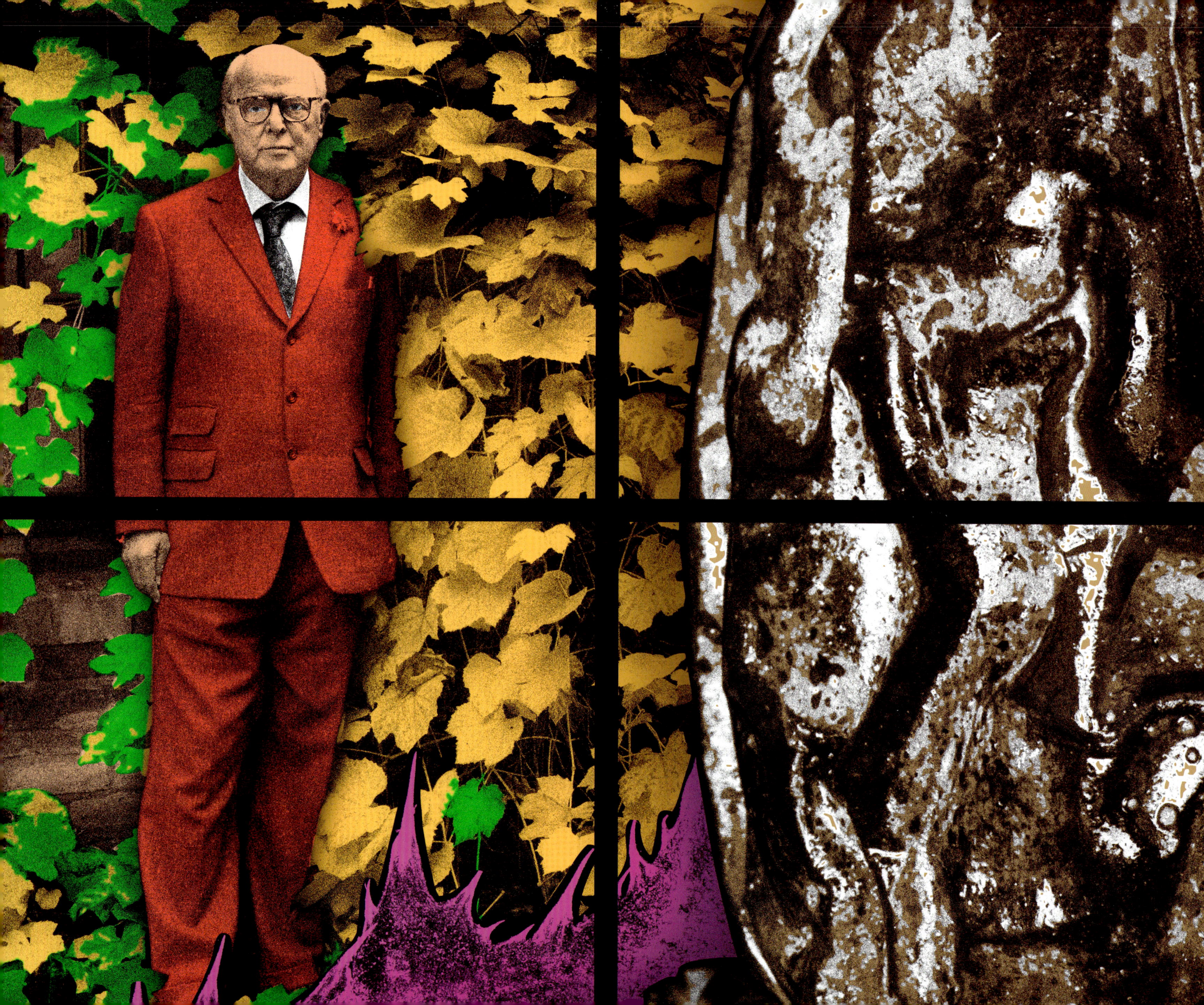

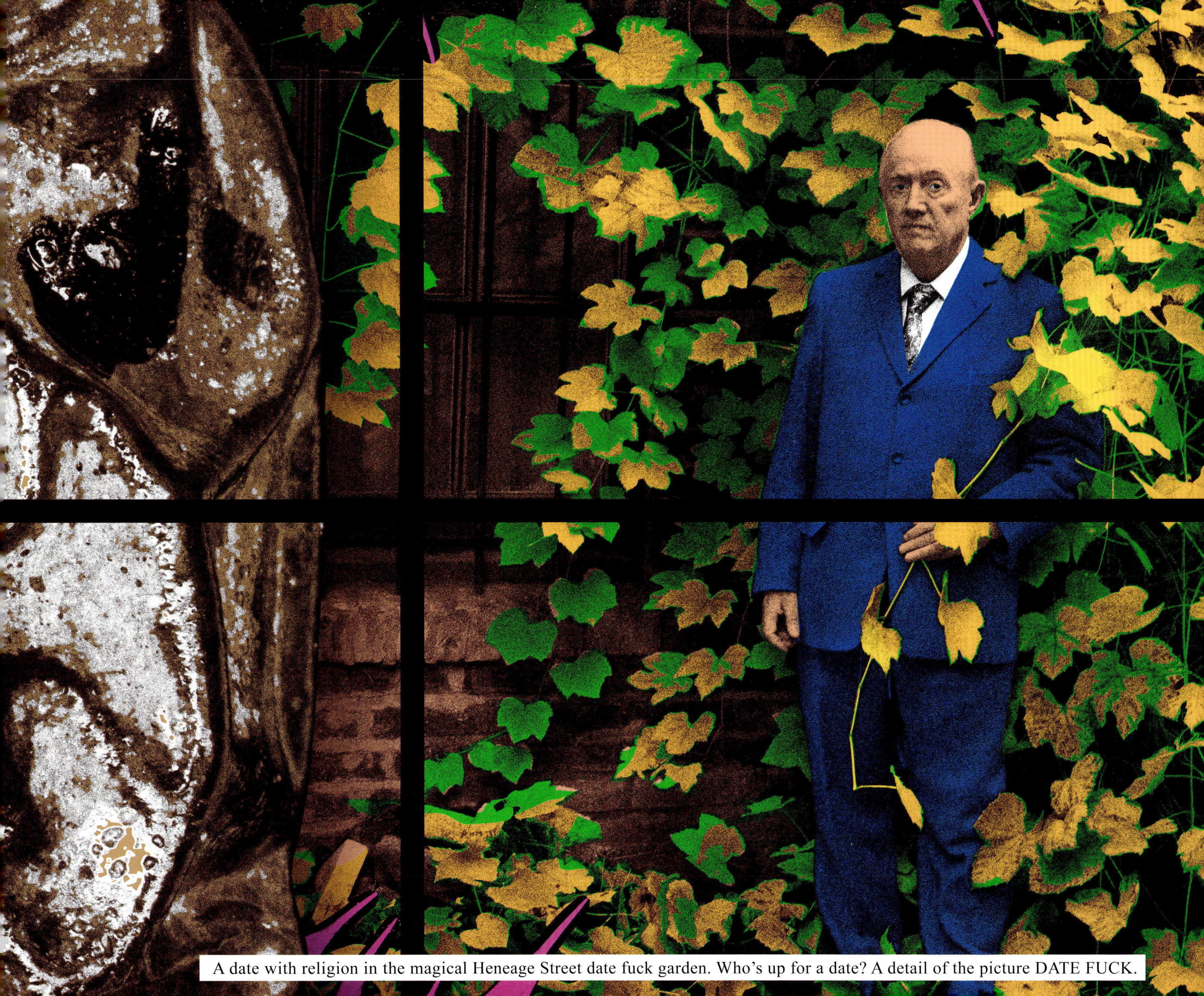

A date with religion in the magical Heneage Street date fuck garden. Who's up for a date? A detail of the picture DATE FUCK.

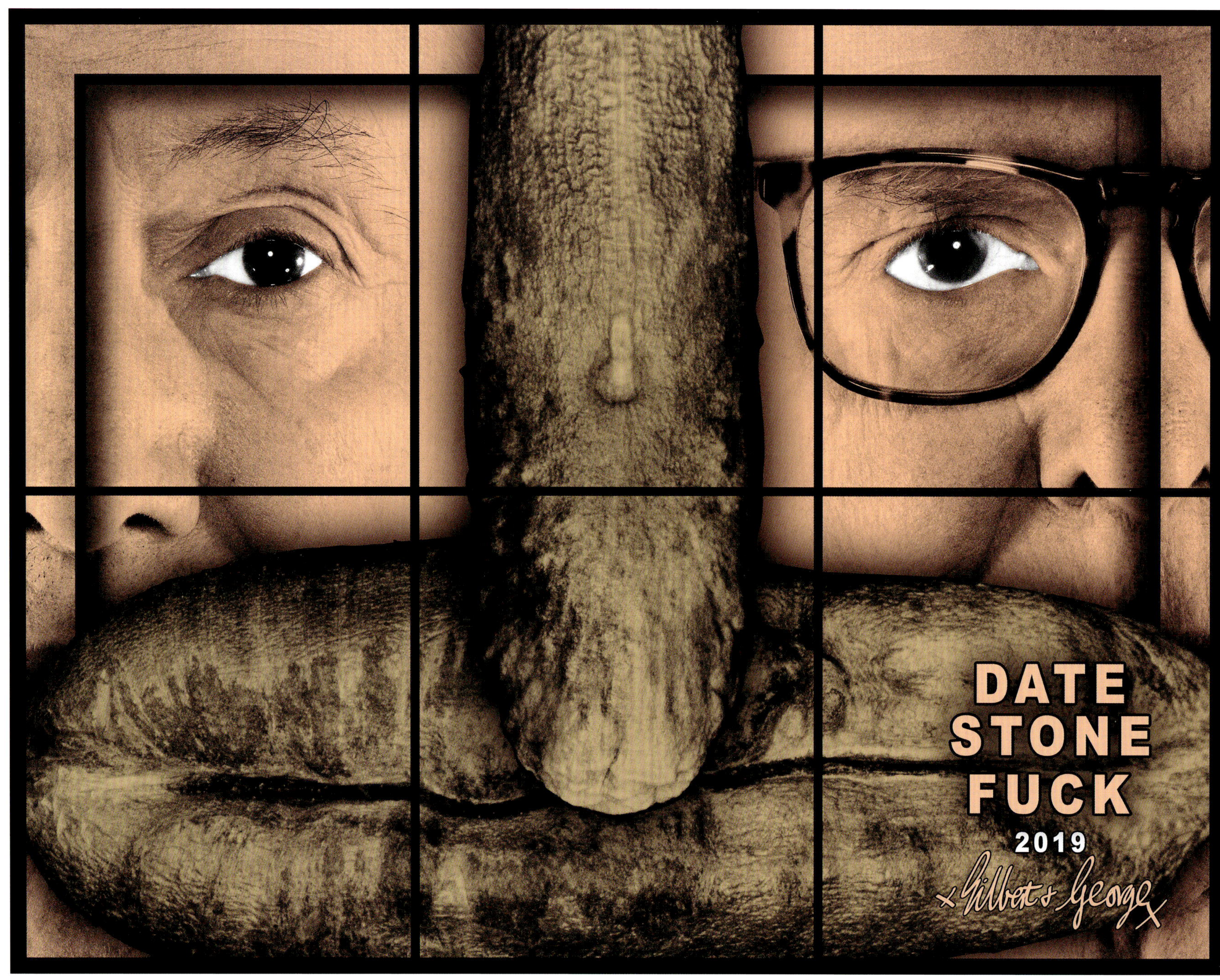

DATE STONE FUCK. 2019. 60 x 75 inches (151 x 190 cm)

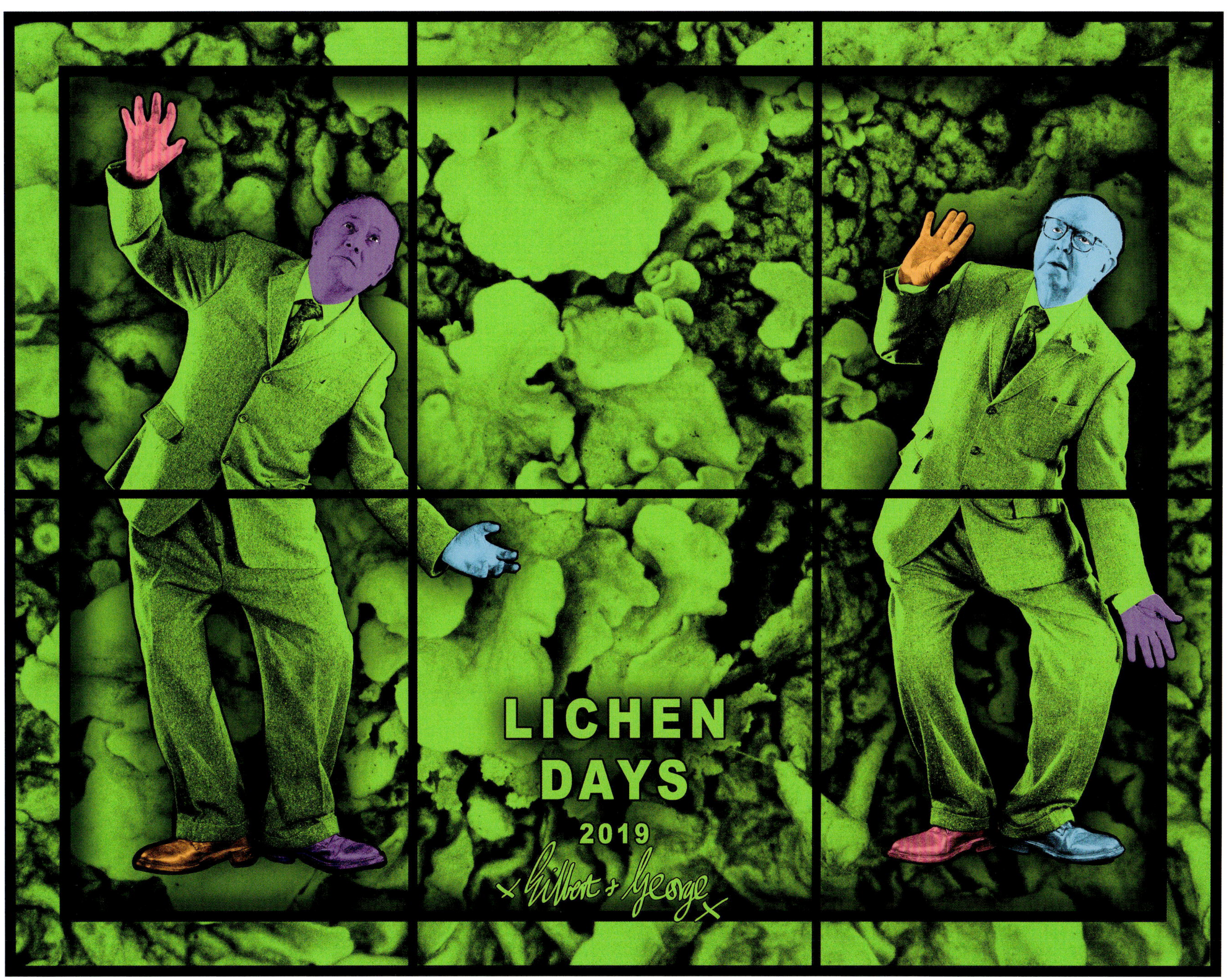

LICHEN DAYS. 2019. 60 x 75 inches (151 x 190 cm)

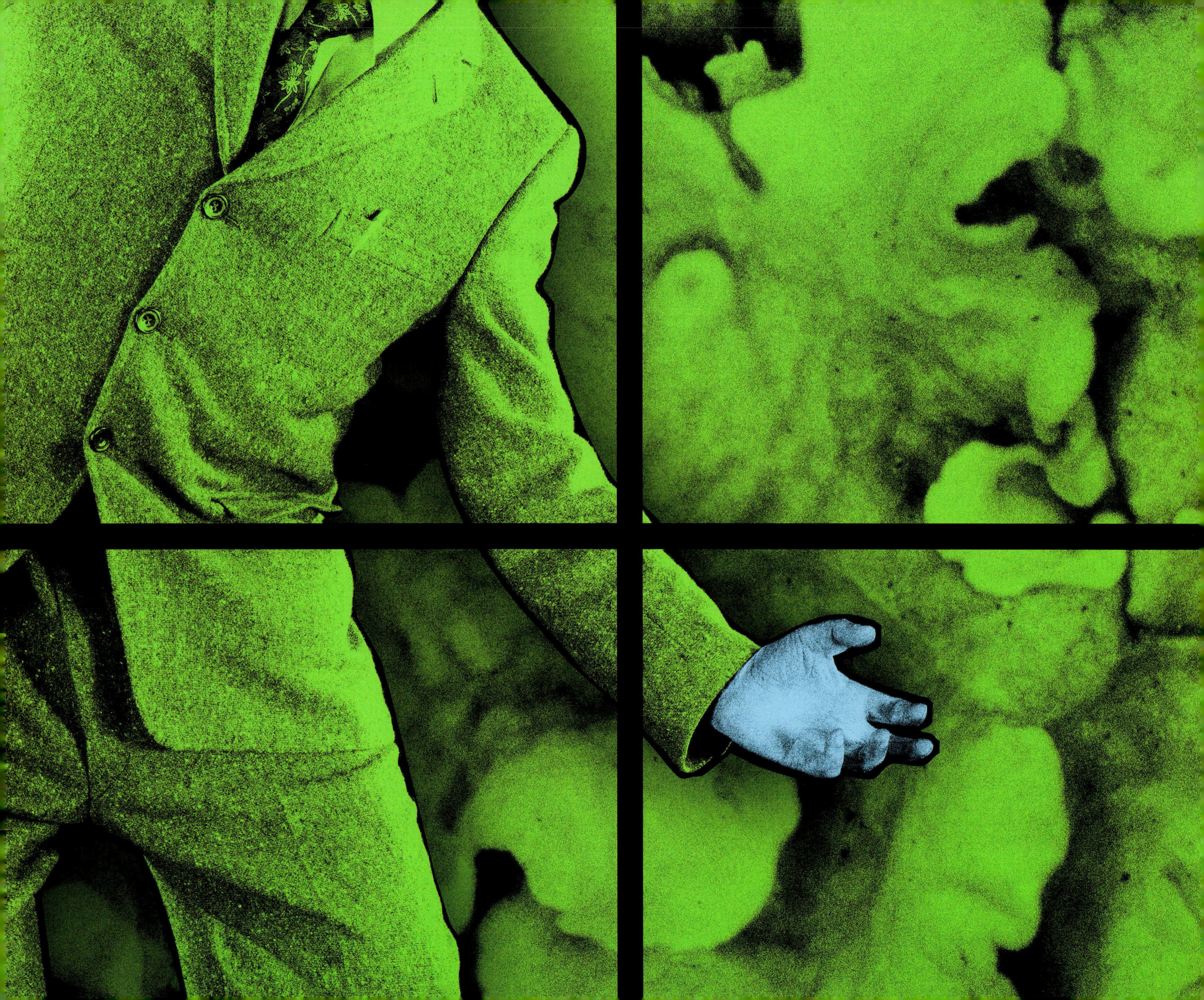

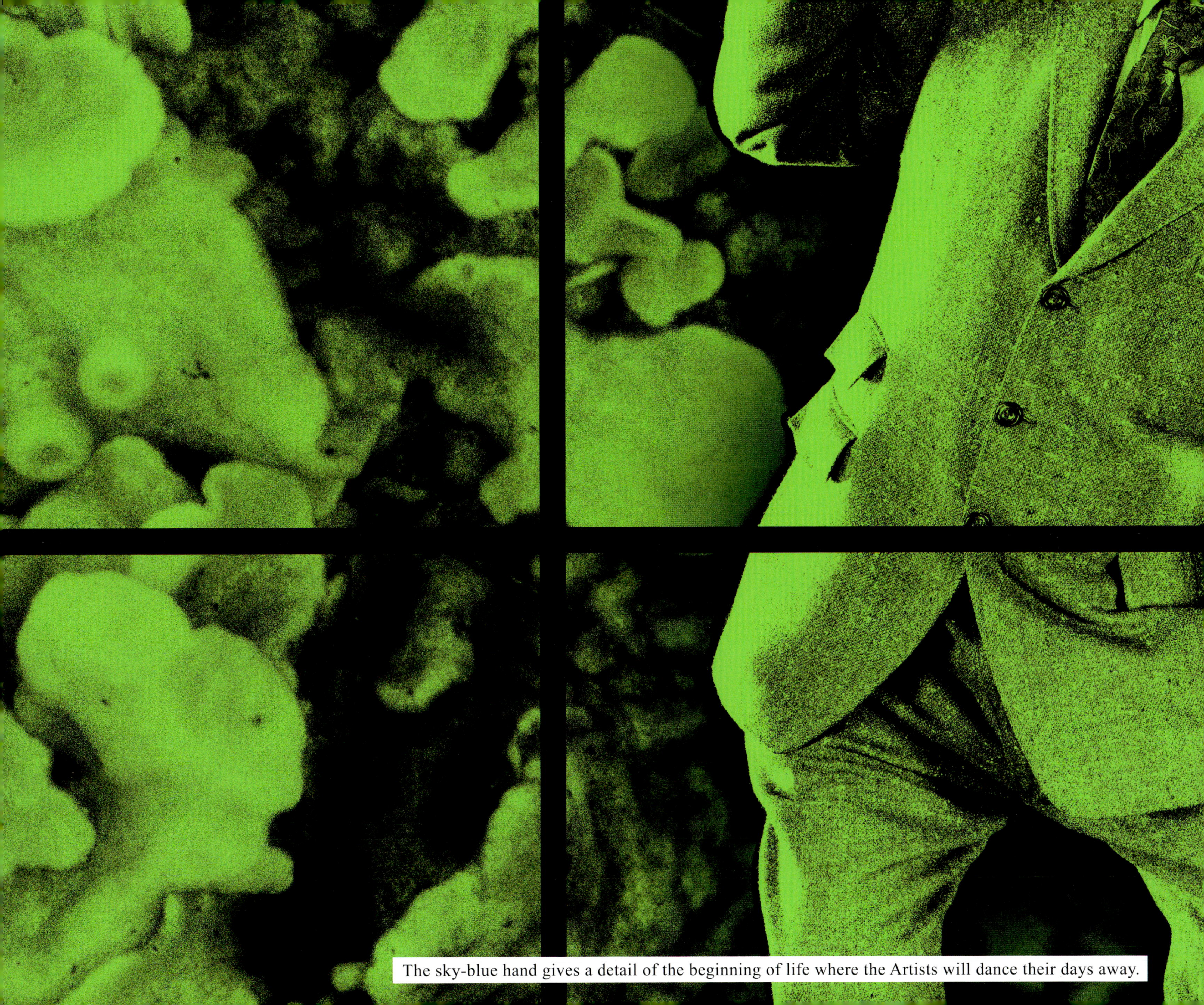

The sky-blue hand gives a detail of the beginning of life where the Artists will dance their days away.

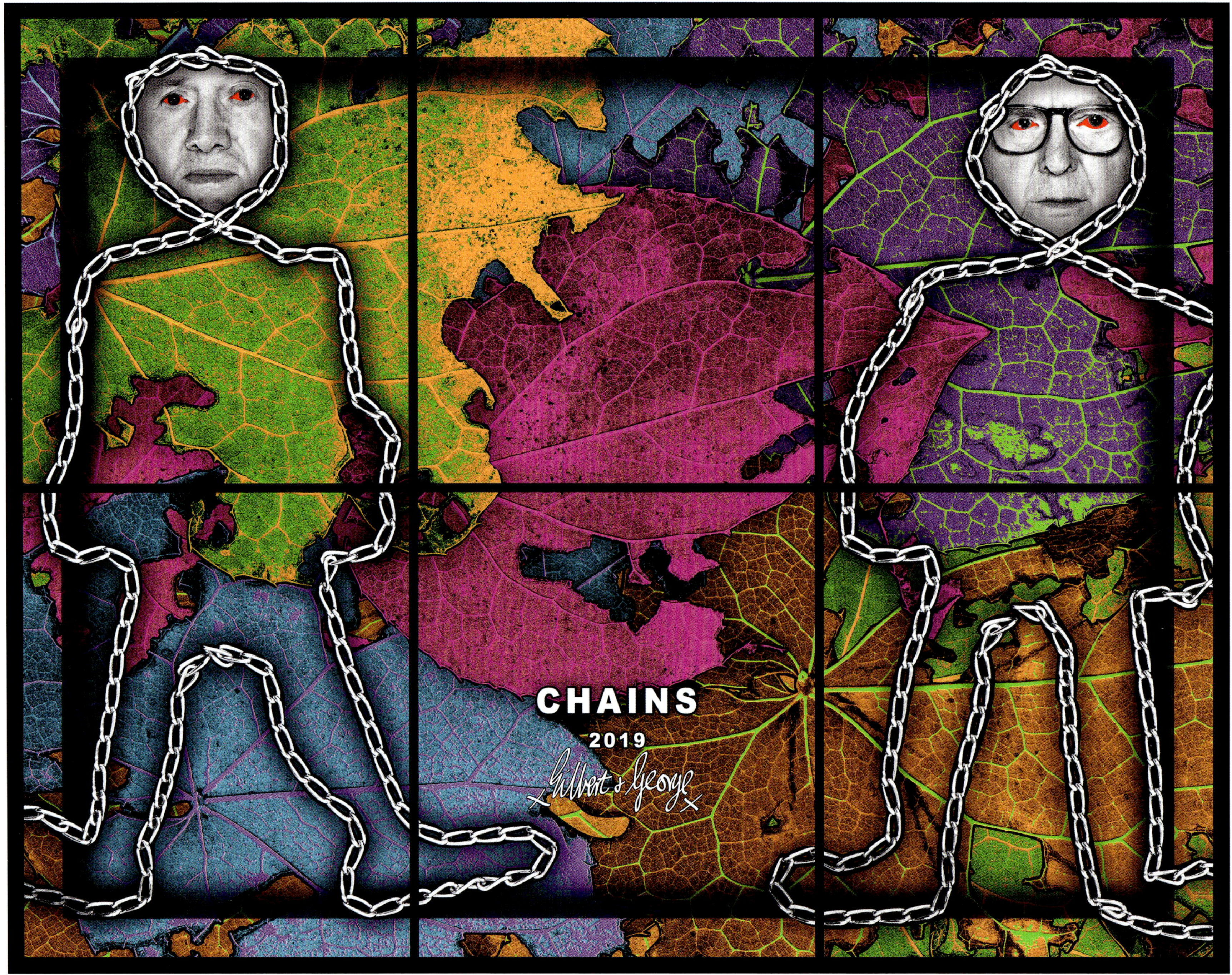

CHAINS. 2019. 60 x 75 inches (151 x 190 cm)

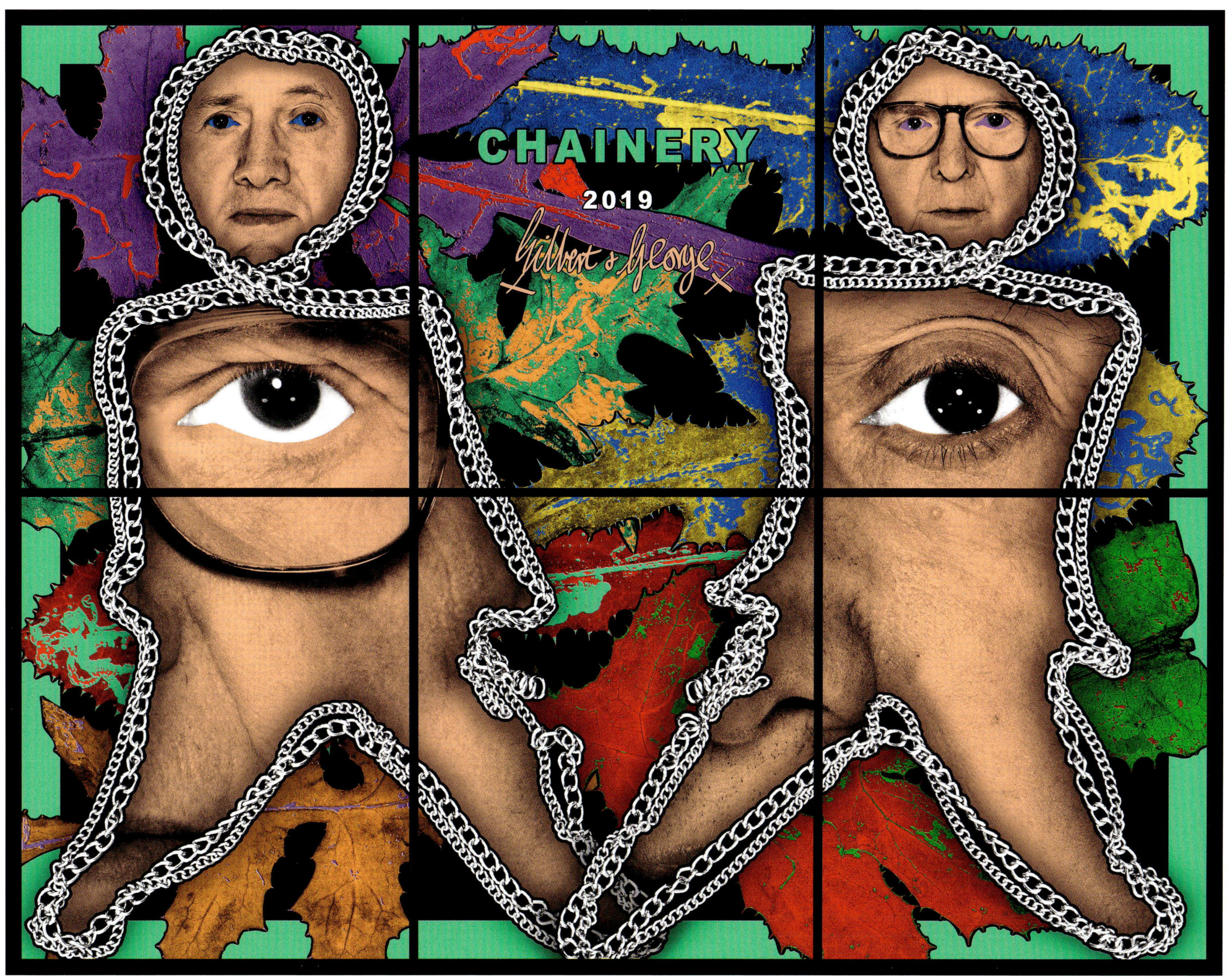

CHAINERY. 2019. 60 x 75 inches (151 x 190 cm)

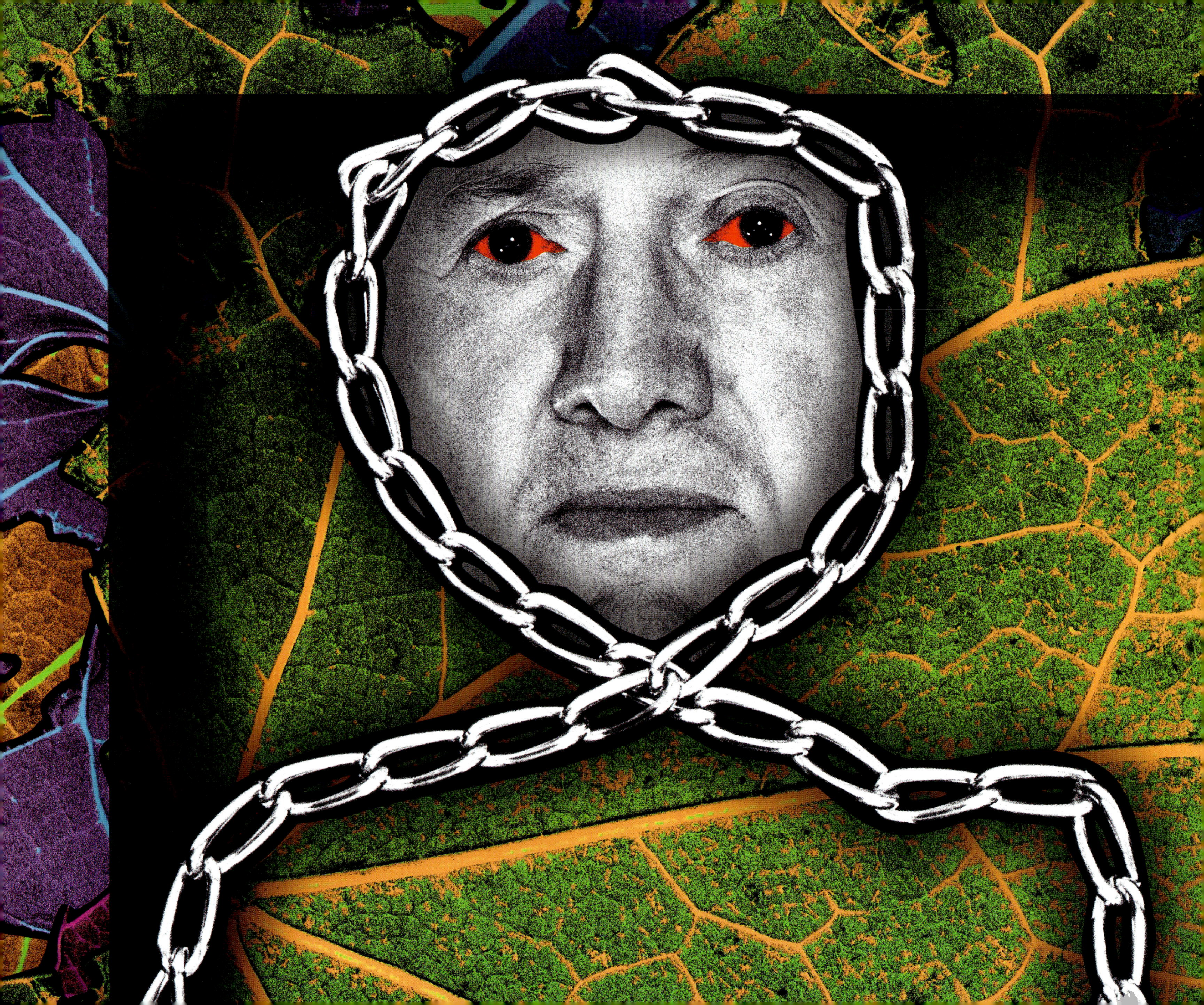

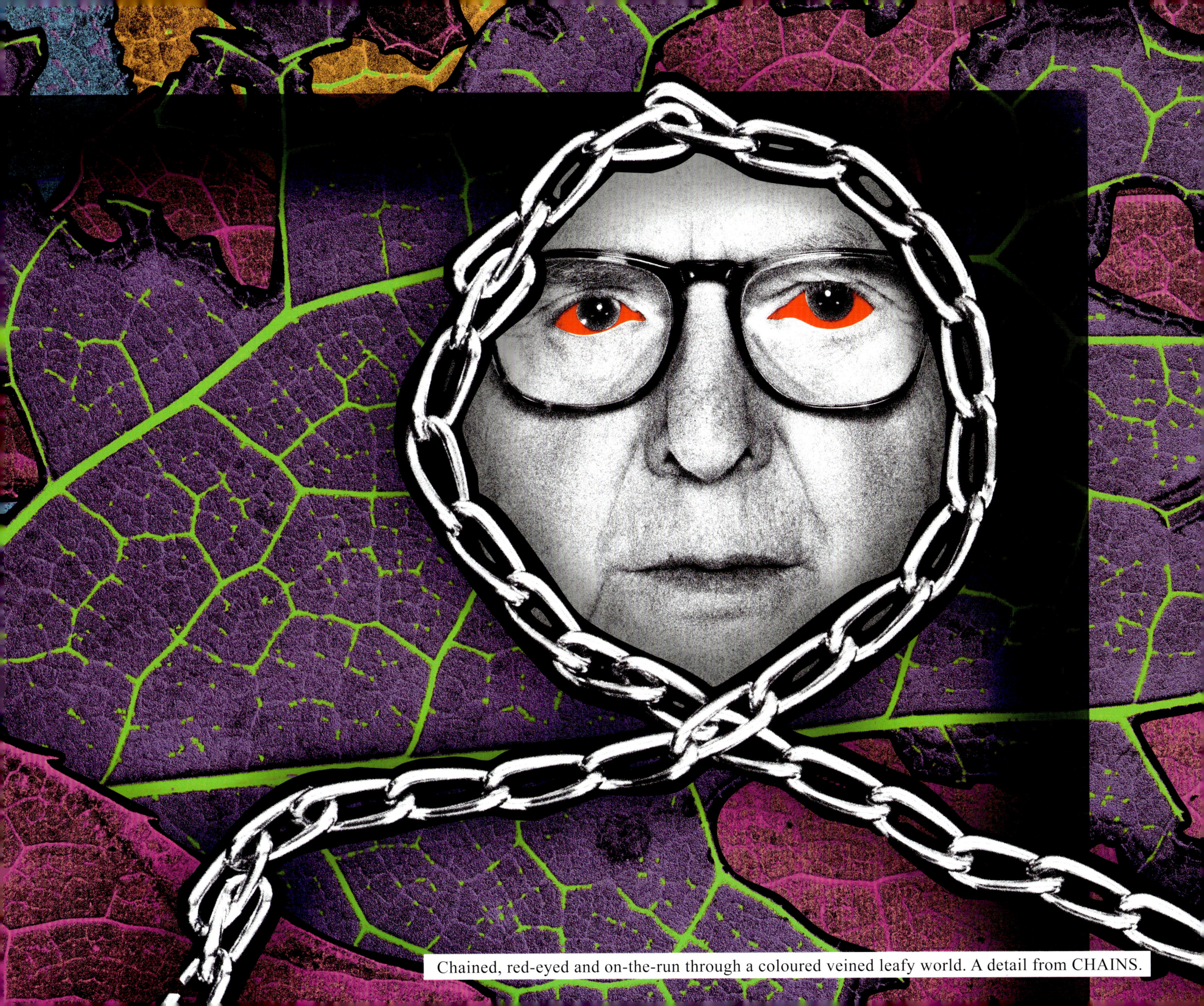

Chained, red-eyed and on-the-run through a coloured veined leafy world. A detail from CHAINS.

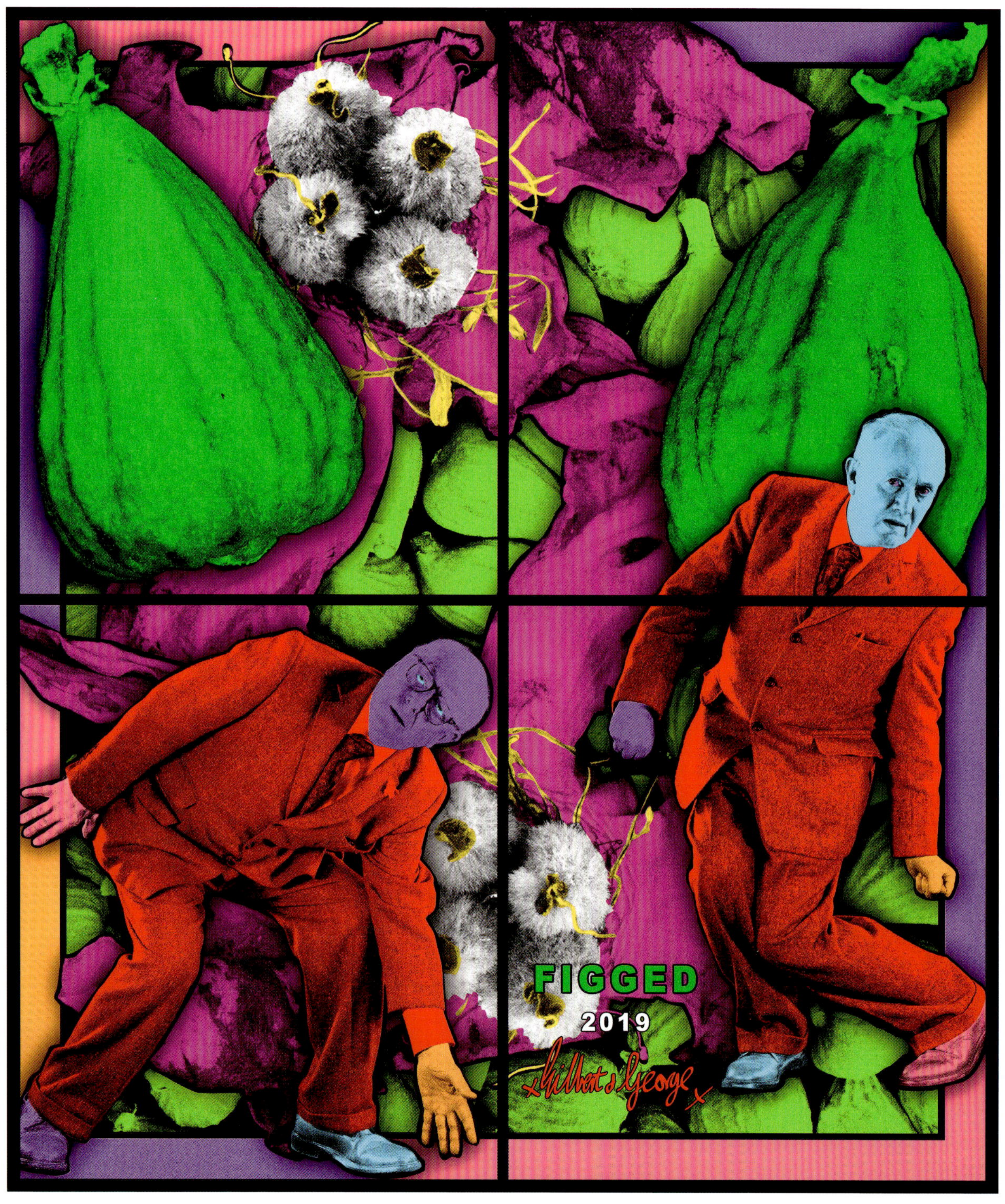

FIGGED. 2019. 60 x 50 inches (151 x 127 cm)

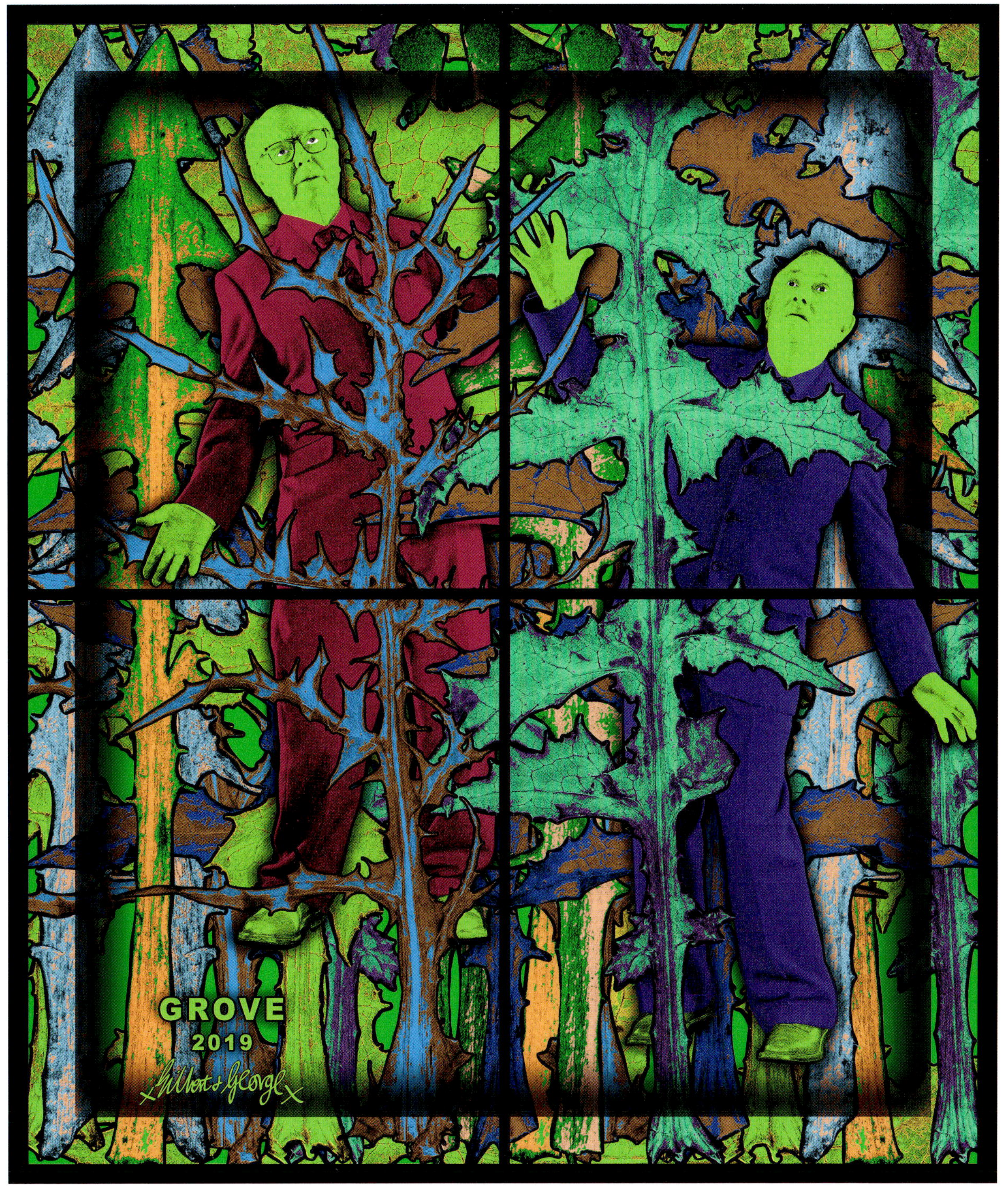

GROVE. 2019. 60 x 50 inches (151 x 127 cm)

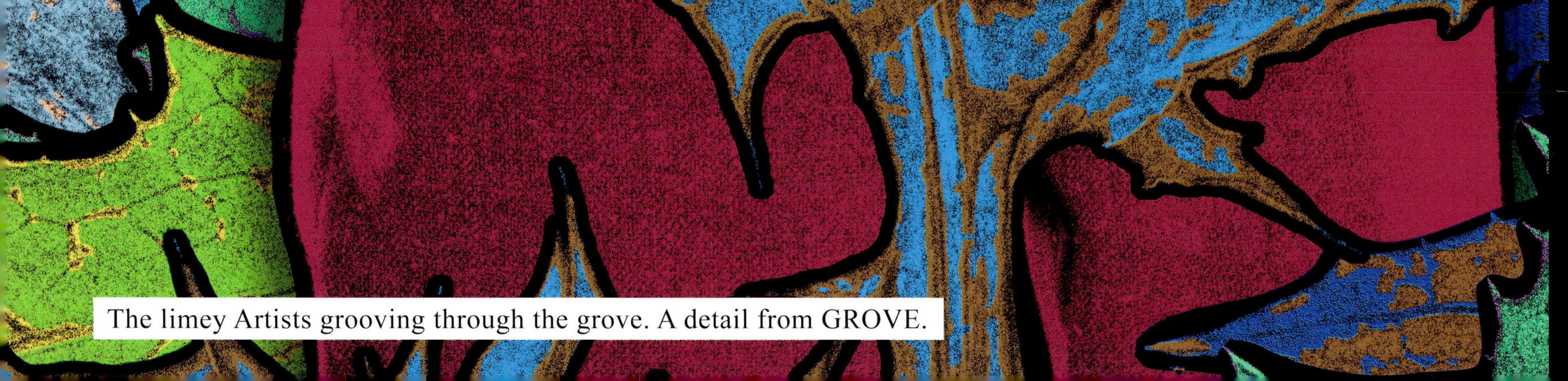
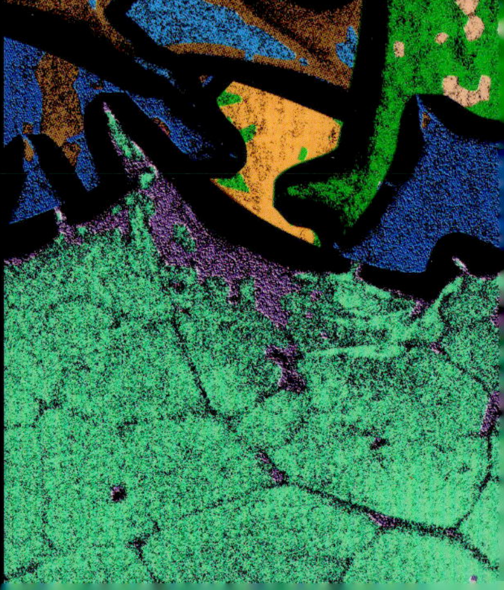

The limey Artists grooving through the grove. A detail from GROVE.

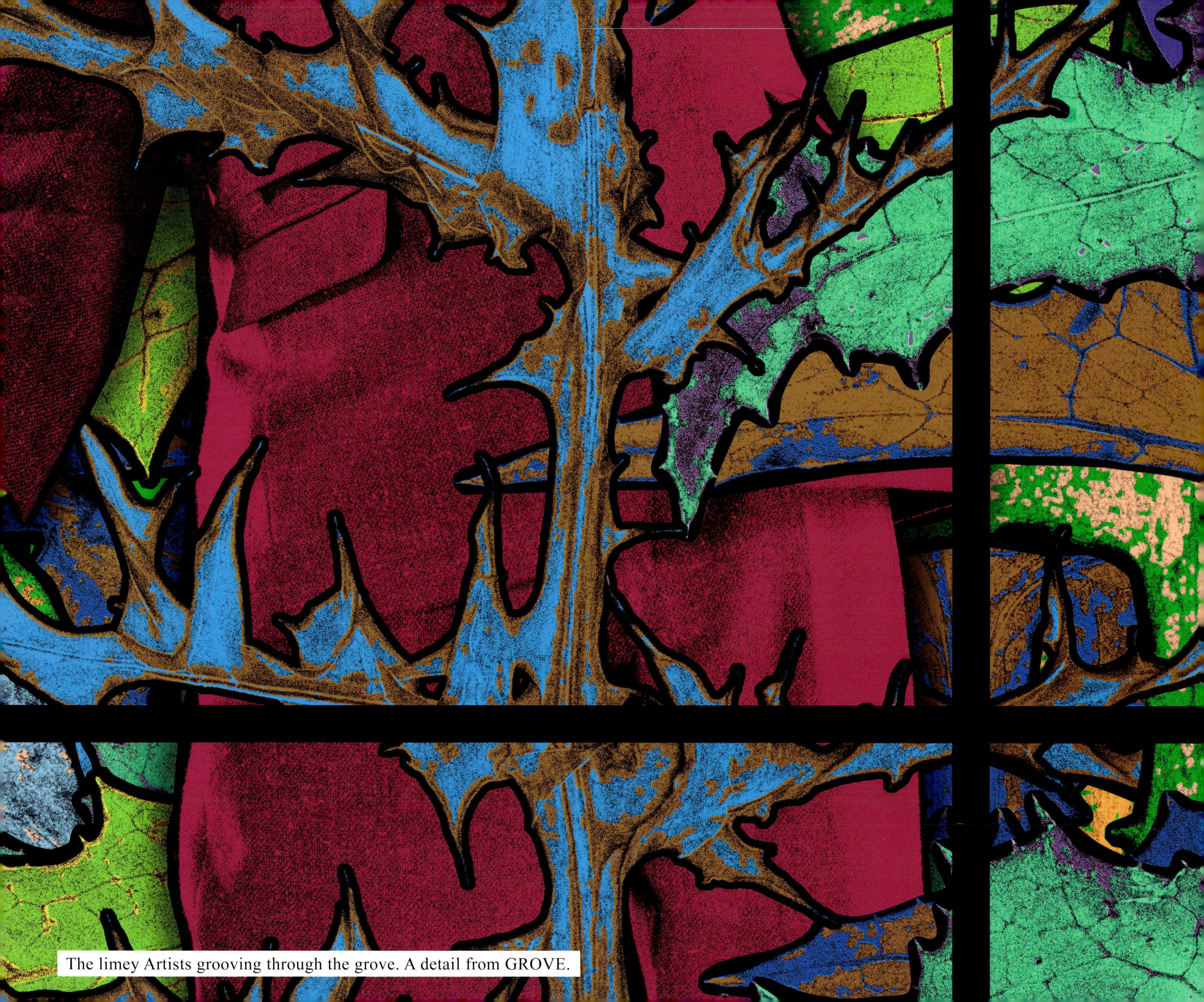

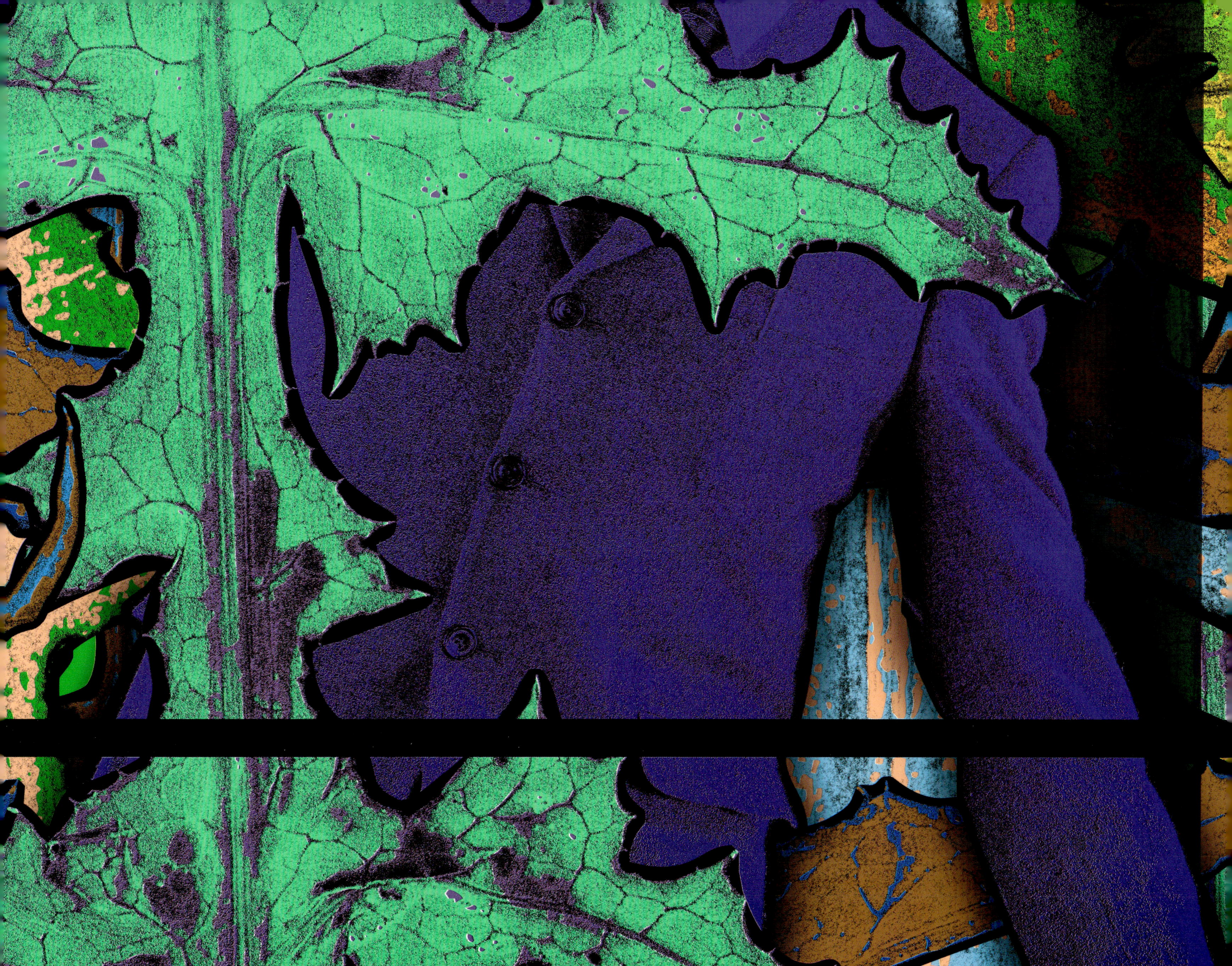

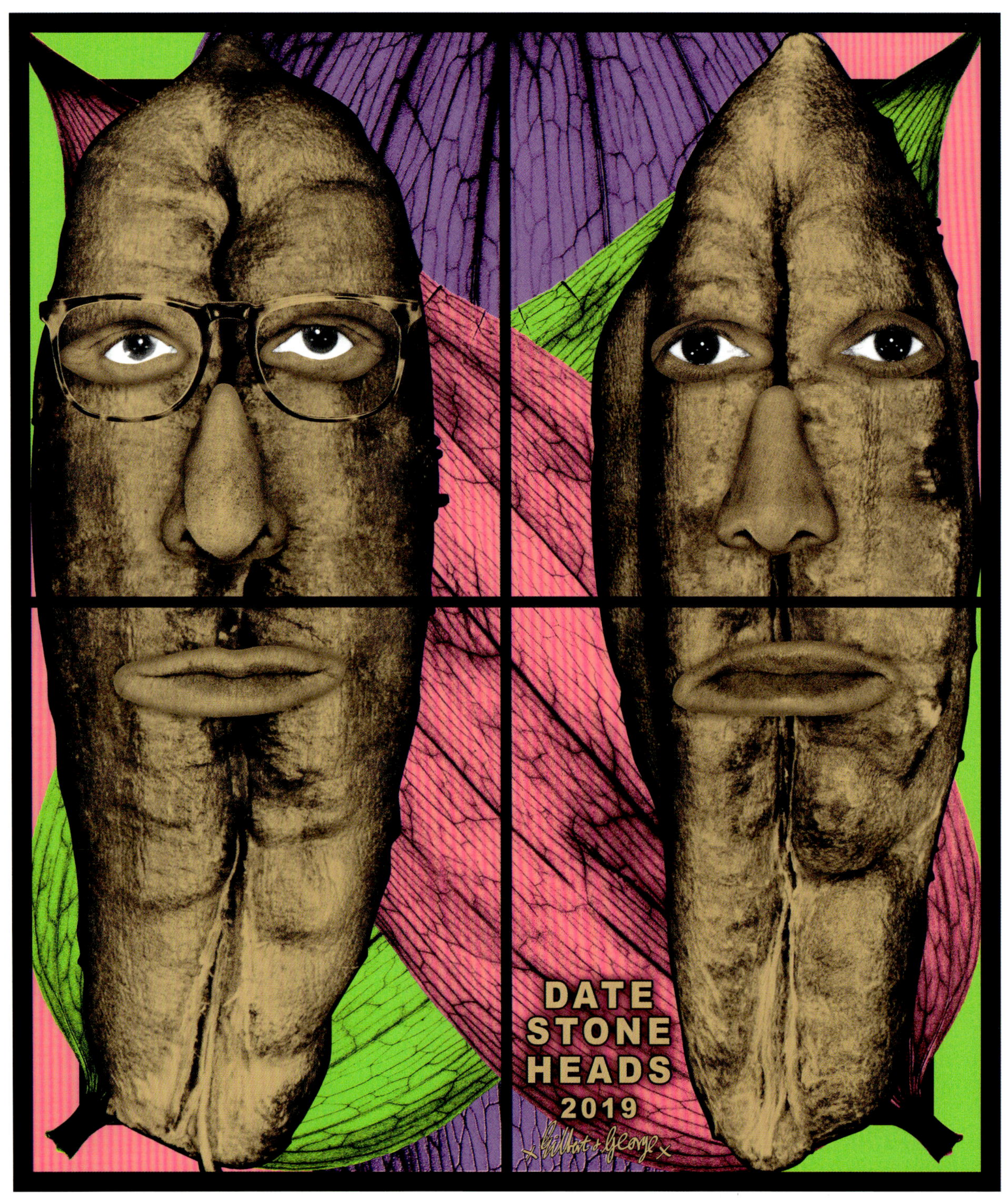

DATE STONE HEADS. 2019. 60 x 50 inches (151 x 127 cm)

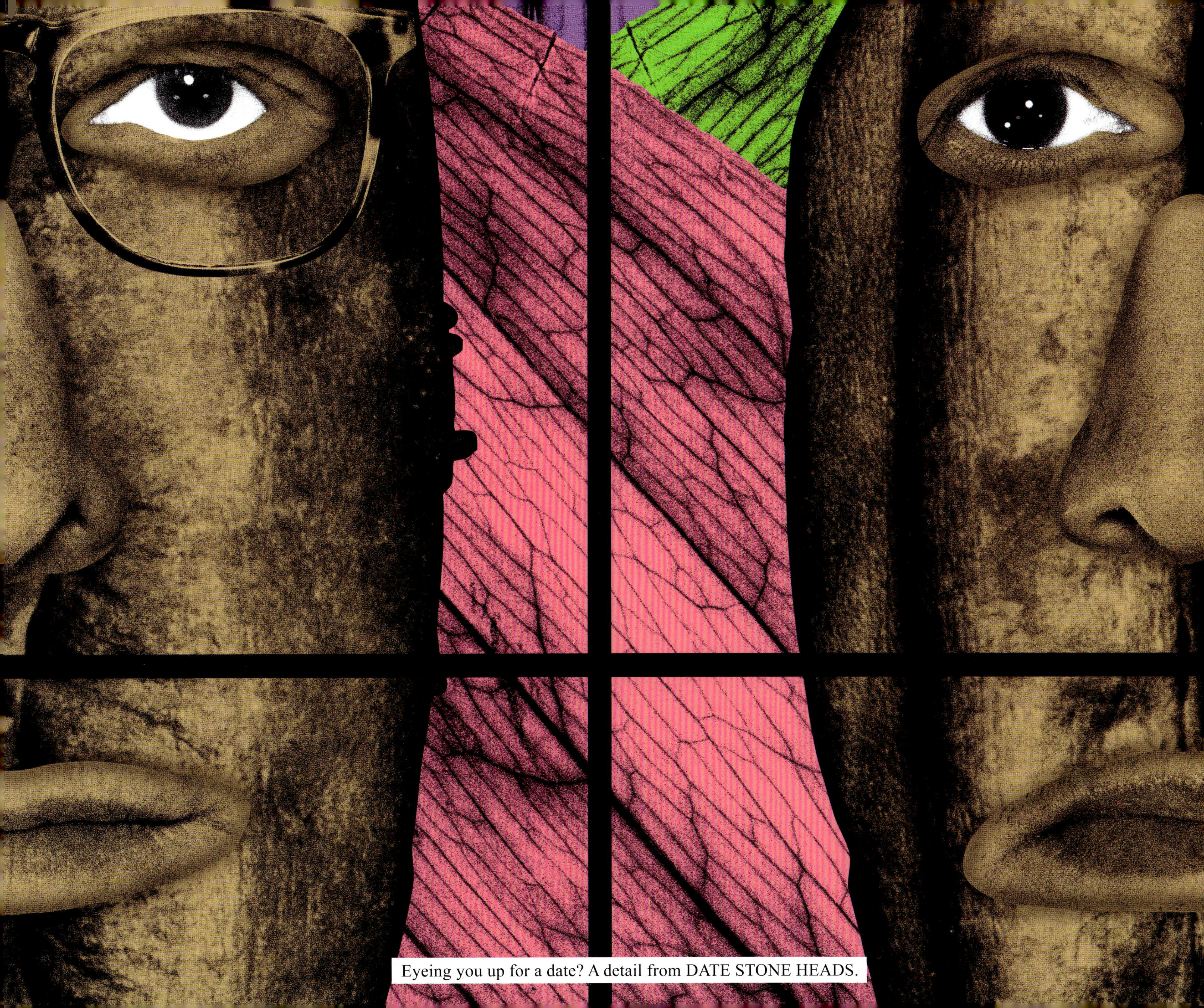

Eyeing you up for a date? A detail from DATE STONE HEADS.

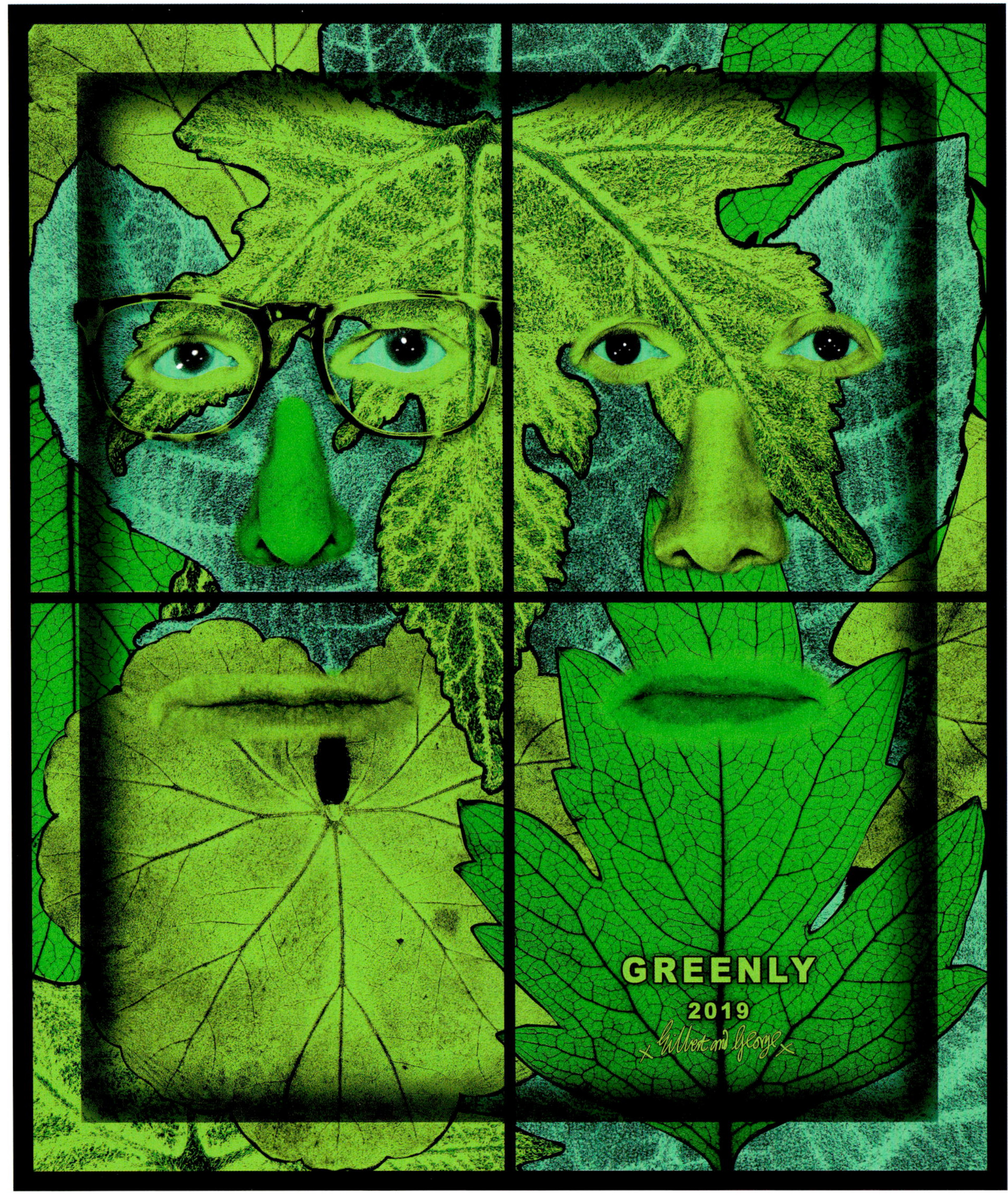

GREENLY. 2019. 60 x 50 inches (151 x 127 cm)

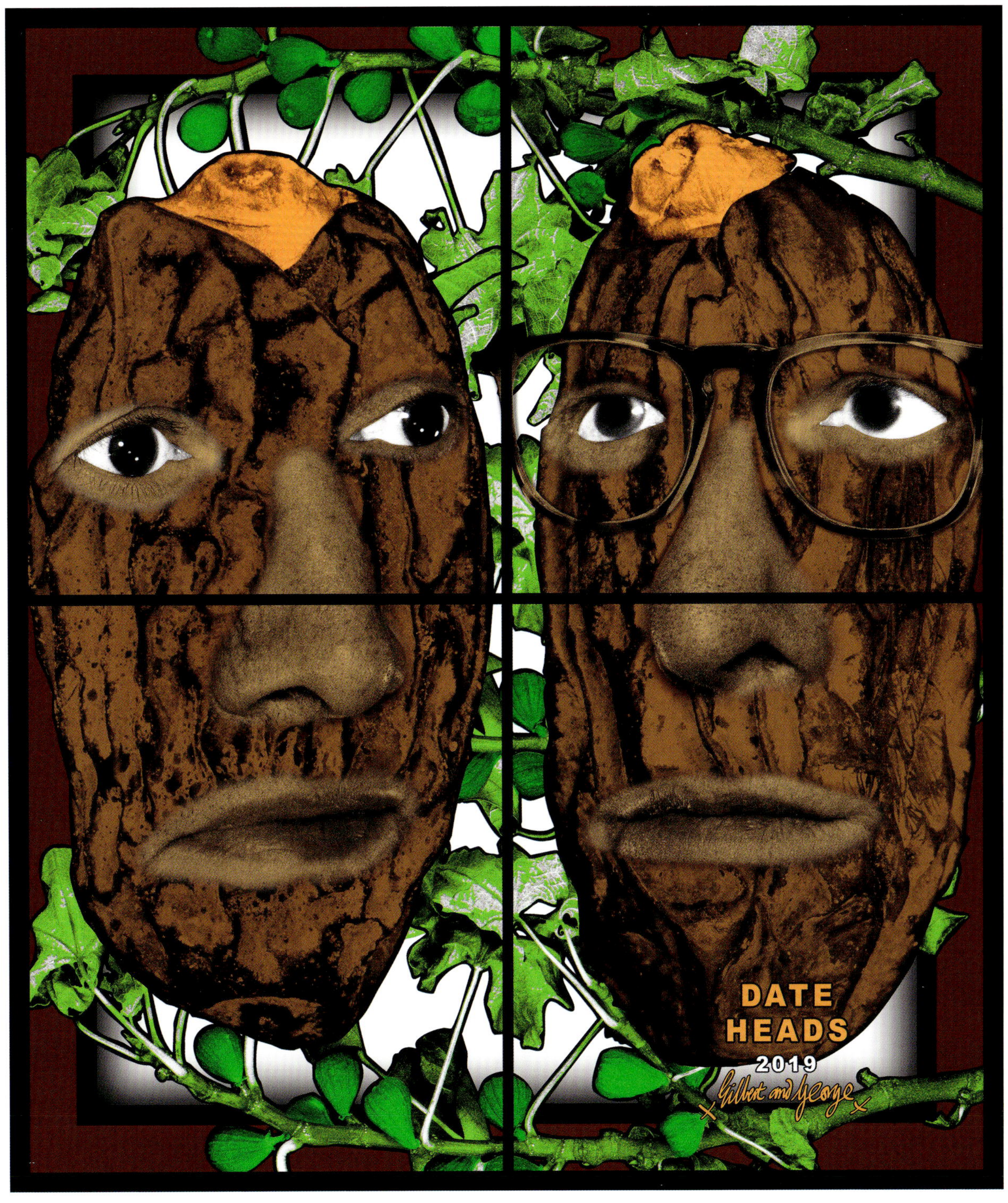

DATE HEADS. 2019. 60 x 50 inches (151 x 127 cm)

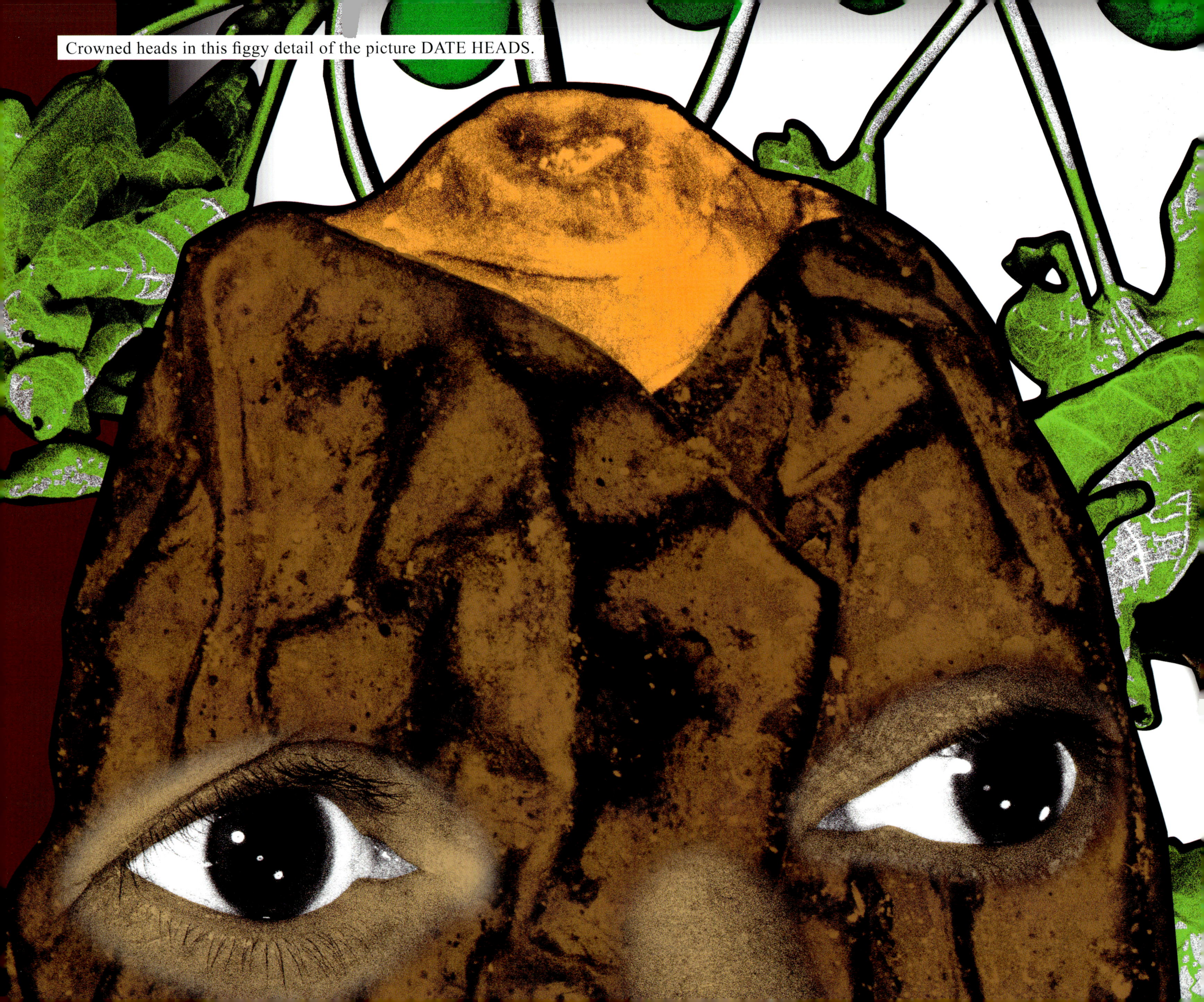

Crowned heads in this figgy detail of the picture DATE HEADS.

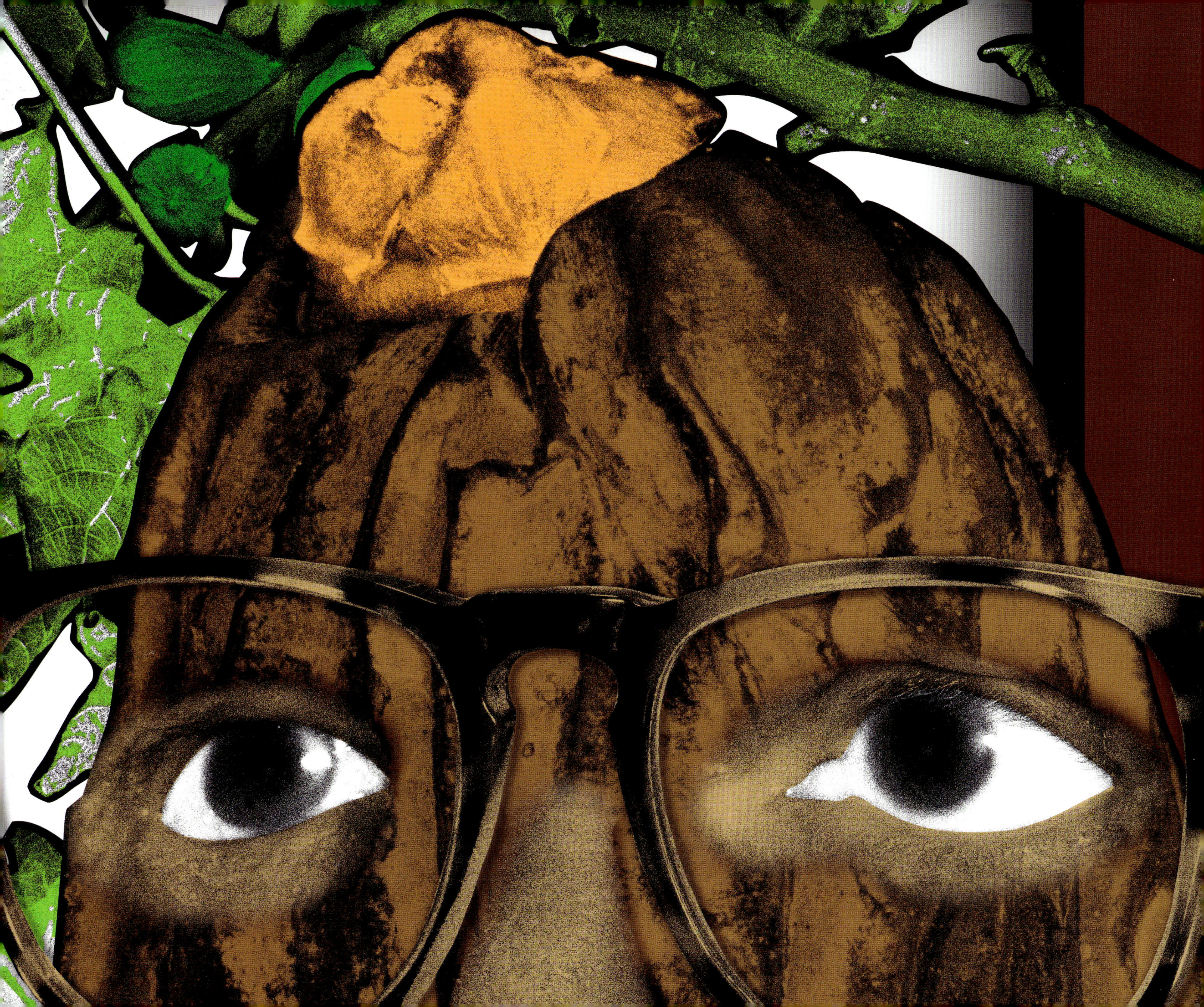

MUSEUM AND PUBLIC GALLERY EXHIBITIONS 1971 to 2023

1971	THE PAINTINGS	Whitechapel Art Gallery, London
1971	THE PAINTINGS	Stedelijk Museum, Amsterdam
1971	THE PAINTINGS	Kunstverein, Düsseldorf
1972	THE PAINTINGS	Koninklijk Museum, Antwerp
1972	THE PAINTINGS	Kunstmuseum, Luzern
1973	THE SHRUBBERIES & SINGING SCULPTURE	National Gallery of NSW (J.Kaldor proj.), Sydney
1973	THE SHRUBBERIES & SINGING SCULPTURE	National Gallery (J.Kaldor proj.), Melbourne
1976	THE GENERAL JUNGLE	Albright-Knox Gallery, Buffalo
1978	PHOTO-PIECES	Dartington Hall Gallery, Dartington
1980	PHOTO-PIECES 1971 – 1980	Van Abbemuseum, Eindhoven
1981	PHOTO-PIECES 1971 – 1980	Kunsthalle, Düsseldorf
1981	PHOTO-PIECES 1971 – 1980	Kunsthalle, Bern
1981	PHOTO-PIECES 1971 – 1980	Pompidou Centre, Paris
1981	PHOTO-PIECES 1971 – 1980	Whitechapel Art Gallery, London
1981	16TH BIENAL DE SAO PAULO	São Paulo
1982	NEW PHOTO-PIECES	Geward, Gent
1984	GILBERT & GEORGE	The Baltimore Museum of Art, Baltimore
1984	GILBERT & GEORGE	Contemporary Arts Museum, Houston
1984	GILBERT & GEORGE	Norton Gallery, West Palm Beach, Florida
1985	GILBERT & GEORGE	Milwaukee Art Museum, Milwaukee
1985	GILBERT & GEORGE	Guggenheim Museum, New York
1986	PICTURES 1982 – 1985	CAPC, Bordeaux
1986	CHARCOAL ON PAPER SCULPTURES 1970 – 1974	CAPC, Bordeaux
1986	THE PAINTINGS 1971	The Fruitmarket, Edinburgh
1986	PICTURES 1982 – 1985	Kunsthalle, Basel
1986	PICTURES 1982 – 1985	Palais des Beaux-Arts, Brussels
1987	PICTURES 1982 – 1985	Palacio de Velasquez, Madrid
1987	PICTURES 1982 – 1985	Lenbachaus, Munich
1987	PICTURES 1982 – 1985	The Hayward Gallery, London
1987	THE 1986 PICTURES	Aldrich Museum, Ridgefield
1990	PICTURES 1983 – 88	Central House of the Artists, Moscow
1991	THE COSMOLOGICAL PICTURES	Palac Sztuki, Krakow
1991	THE COSMOLOGICAL PICTURES	Palazzo delle Esposizioni, Rome
1992	THE COSMOLOGICAL PICTURES	Kunsthalle, Zürich
1992	THE COSMOLOGICAL PICTURES	Wiener Secession, Vienna
1992	THE COSMOLOGICAL PICTURES	Ernst Múzeum, Budapest
1992	THE COSMOLOGICAL PICTURES	Haags Gemeentemusem, The Hague
1992	NEW DEMOCRATIC PICTURES	Aarhus Kunstmuseum, Aarhus
1992	THE COSMOLOGICAL PICTURES	Irish Museum of Modern Art, Dublin
1992	THE COSMOLOGICAL PICTURES	Fundació Joan Miró, Barcelona
1993	THE COSMOLOGICAL PICTURES	Tate Gallery, Liverpool
1993	THE COSMOLOGICAL PICTURES	Württembergischer Kunstverein, Stuttgart
1993	GILBERT & GEORGE CHINA EXHIBITION	National Art Gallery, Beijing
1993	GILBERT & GEORGE CHINA EXHIBITION	The Art Museum, Shanghai
1994	RETROSPECTIVE	Museo d'Arte Moderna, Lugano
1994	SHITTY NAKED HUMAN WORLD	Wolfsburg Kunstmuseum, Wolfsburg
1995	THE NAKED SHIT PICTURES	South London Gallery, London
1996	THE NAKED SHIT PICTURES	Stedelijk Museum, Amsterdam
1996	GILBERT & GEORGE RETROSPECTIVE	Galleria d'Arte Moderna, Bologna
1997	GILBERT & GEORGE RETROSPECTIVE	Sezon Museum, Tokyo
1997	PICTURES 1991 – 1996	Magasin 3, Stockholm
1997	GILBERT & GEORGE RETROSPECTIVE	Musée d'Art Moderne de la Ville, Paris
1998	NEW TESTAMENTAL PICTURES	Museo di Capodimonte, Naples
1999	GILBERT & GEORGE 1970 – 1988	Astrup Fearnley Museet, Oslo
1999	PICTURES 1986 – 1997	Drassanes, Valencia
1999	PICTURES 1991 – 1997	Ormeau Baths Gallery, Belfast
1999	THE RUDIMENTARY PICTURES	Milton Keynes Gallery, Milton Keynes
1999	NINETEEN NINETY NINE	Kunstmuseum, Bonn
2000	NINETEEN NINETY NINE	Museum Moderner Kunst, Vienna
2000	NINETEEN NINETY NINE	Museum of Contemporary Art, Chicago
2000	MM 2000, BIENNALE DE LYON	Halle Tony Garnier, Lyon
2001	GILBERT & GEORGE	Chateau d'Arenton, Alex
2001	THE ART OF GILBERT & GEORGE	The Factory, Athens School of Art, Athens
2002	THE DIRTY WORDS PICTURES	Serpentine Gallery, London
2002	NINE DARK PICTURES	Portikus, Frankfurt
2002	GILBERT & GEORGE	Centro Cultural de Belém, Lisbon
2002	GILBERT & GEORGE	Kunsthaus Bregenz, Austria
2004	TWENTY LONDON EAST ONE PICTURES	Musee d'Art Moderne, Saint-Etienne
2005	GINKGO PICTURES	Venice Biennale, Venice
2005	TWENTY LONDON EAST ONE PICTURES	Kestnergesellschaft, Hanover
2006	SONOFAGOD PICTURES: Was Jesus Heterosexual?	Bonnefanten Museum, Maastricht
2007	MAJOR EXHIBITION	Tate Modern, London
2007	MAJOR EXHIBITION	Haus der Kunst, Munich
2007	MAJOR EXHIBITION	Castello di Rivoli, Turin
2008	MAJOR EXHIBITION	Milwaukee Art Museum, Milwaukee
2008	MAJOR EXHIBITION	De Young Museum, San Francisco
2008	MAJOR EXHIBITION	Brooklyn Museum, New York
2008	NOTATIONS: GILBERT AND GEORGE	Philadelphia Museum of Art, Philadelphia
2010	JACK FREAK PICTURES	Centro de Arte Contemporãneo, Malaga
2010	JACK FREAK PICTURES	Museum of Contemporary Art, Zagreb
2010	THE PAINTINGS (WITH US IN NATURE) 1971	Kröller-Müller Museum, Otterlo
2010	JACK FREAK PICTURES	The Centre for Fine Arts, Brussels
2011	JACK FREAK PICTURES	Deichtorhallen, Hamburg
2011	JACK FREAK PICTURES	Lentos Art Museum, Linz
2011	THE URETHRA POSTCARD PICTURES	Ivorypress Art + Books, Madrid
2011	JACK FREAK PICTURES	Laznia Centre for Contemporary Art, Gdańsk
2011	THE URETHRA POSTCARD PICTURES	Pinacotela Giovanni e Marella Agnelli, Torino
2013	LONDON PICTURES	Museum Küppersmühle, Duisburg
2013	LONDON PICTURES	Casal Solleric, Palma
2014	A FAMILY COLLECTION	NMNM - Villa Paloma, Monaco
2015	GILBERT & GEORGE: THE EARLY YEARS	MOMA, New York
2015	GILBERT & GEORGE: THE ART EXHIBITION	MONA, Tasmania
2017	THE SCAPEGOATING PICTURES BERLIN	St. Matthaüs Church Berlin
2017	SCAPEGOATING PICTURES	Ludwig museum, Budapest
2018	SCAPEGOATING PICTURES	The MAC, Belfast
2018	THE GREAT EXHIBITION	LUMA, Arles
2018	GILBERT & GEORGE MAJOR EXHIBITION	HAM, Helsinki
2019	THE GREAT EXHIBITION	Moderna Museet, Stockholm
2019	THE GREAT EXHIBITION	Astrup Fearnley Museet, Oslo
2020	THE GREAT EXHIBITION	LUMA Westbau + Kunsthalle Zurich, Zurich
2020	THE LOCARNO EXHIBITION	Pinacoteca Comunale Casa Rusca
2020	THE GREAT EXHIBITION	Reykjavik Art Museum, Iceland
2021	THE GREAT EXHIBITION	Schirn Kunsthalle, Frankfurt
2022	THE AUCKLAND EXHIBITION	Auckland Art Gallery, New Zealand

INDEX TO PARADISICAL PICTURE TITLES

Published to accompany the inaugural exhibition at

THE GILBERT AND GEORGE CENTRE

5a Heneage Street, London E1 5LJ

THE PARADISICAL PICTURES
LONDON 2023

Published by Hurtwood Press, SB113, 100 Black Prince Road, London SE1 7SJ

ISBN 978-0-903696-59-3 (Hardback)
ISBN 978-0-903696-70-8 (Softback)

Printed and bound in Italy

THE GILBERT AND GEORGE CENTRE
www.gilbertandgeorgecentre.org